笔墨纸砚

Writing Brush, Ink Stick, Paper and Ink Slab

季孙歆 ◎ 编著

全国百佳图书出版单位

时代出版传媒股份有限公司

黄山书社

图书在版编目(CIP)数据

笔墨纸砚：汉英对照 / 季孙歇编著. ——合肥：
黄山书社, 2011.11
　（中国红）
　ISBN 978-7-5461-2273-1

　Ⅰ.①笔… Ⅱ.①季… Ⅲ.①文化用品—介绍—
中国—汉、英 Ⅳ.①K875.4

中国版本图书馆CIP数据核字(2011)第215897号

笔墨纸砚　　　　　　　　　　　　　　　　　　季孙歇 编著

责任编辑：范丽娜　　　　　　　　　　　　　特约编辑：朱昌爱
责任印制：戚　帅　李　磊　　　　　　　　　装帧设计：商子庄

出版发行：时代出版传媒股份有限公司（http://www.press-mart.com）
　　　　　黄山书社（http://www.hsbook.cn）
　　　　　（合肥市蜀山区翡翠路1118号出版传媒广场7层　邮编：230071）
经　　销：新华书店　　　　　　　　　　营销电话：0551-3533762　3533768
印　　刷：合肥精艺印刷有限公司　　　　　电　话：0551-4859368

开　　本：710×875　1/16　　　　印张：12　　　　字数：149千字
版　　次：2012年1月第1版　　2012年1月第1次印刷
书　　号：ISBN 978-7-5461-2273-1　　　　　定价：59.00元

笔、墨、纸、砚是中国古代文房用具中的代表，被历代中国文人视为至宝。它们不仅是中国古代书画艺术的载体和组成部分，也体现着中国古代文人的生活情趣。

在中国五千年的历史长河中，中国人不断开拓创新，形成了自己独特的文化传承体系。作为中国传统文化的代表性符号之一的笔、墨、纸、砚，凝聚着传统文化的精髓，它们不仅演绎出中国古代书画艺术的神韵，记录下了华夏民族的辉煌历史，其本身也闪耀着独特的

Traditionally, ink stick, ink slab, paper and writing brush were four treasures of Chinese scholars. They were often used collectively referring to their study. These four were indispensable in writing, painting and calligraphy doing, also something to show a refined taste.

Over the past five thousand years, by continuous efforts to innovate and invent, Chinese nation created a brilliant culture. Ink sticks, ink slabs, paper and writing brushes, often used as the logo of this culture, made four unique blooms in the garden of Chinese civilization. With the four, Chinese calligraphic and painting art flourished and Chinese history was recorded. These four were no longer only tools; they became works of art . Even today, their role is vital to Chinese painting and calligraphy.

艺术光芒。今天，笔、墨、纸、砚仍然在中国传统书画创作中发挥着重要的作用，是现代文具中一道亮丽的风景线。

本书以中英文对照的形式，配以大量精美图片，向海内外读者分别展示了笔、墨、纸、砚的发展历程、品种以及收藏名品，希望能够带领读者了解中国书房文化、体会不同文房用具的艺术魅力。

With text in Chinese and English and fabulous illustrations and photos this book is an attempt made to probe into their origin, styles, famous varieties to collectors and the road they have taken. This book, we hope, is able to usher you into a fascinating culture related to a book reader's study and fascinating things they used in history.

目 录 Contents

笔墨纸砚——中国人的文房四宝

Writing Brush, Ink Stick, Paper and Ink Slab——Collectively Called "Four Treasures of a Chinese Study"

　　笔、墨、纸、砚合称"文房四宝"，是四种中国古代的文房用具。"文房"原指官府掌管文书的部门，后来专指文人的书房。最先把笔、墨、纸、砚称为"文房四宝"的是北宋的苏易简，他在其所作《文房四谱》中对笔、墨、纸、砚进行了详细的论述，"文房四宝"由此得名。

These four treasures referring to ink sticks, ink slabs, paper and writing brushes a scholar in the old days kept in his study. "Study" in Chinese was "*wen fang*", which originally meant governmental departments in charge of record making and keeping. Later, this word became exclusively for book readers' study, nothing else. The first one in history who ever used the phrase "the four treasures of the study" was Su Yijian of the Northern Song Dynasty. In his writing *Wen Fang Si Pu* or *The Four Treasures of the Study*, he detailed each of them. Thus the phrase was born.

文房四宝中，除纸出现稍晚外，笔、墨、砚都有着悠久的历史。在这漫长的发展过程中，文房四宝的制作水平与日俱增，涌现了不少名工巧匠。他们精选名材，施展精湛的技艺，创造了大量的文房精品，为中国传统文化留下了灿烂的遗产。

笔、墨、纸、砚是中国古代文人必备的文房用具，因此其几千年的发展都是在古代文人的关注与参与下进行的。从器形到纹饰，从选材到制作，都凝结着古代文人的文化素养和审美观念。

Apart from paper that came later, all the rest three have a long history behind, during which time their making technology was perfected and master makers appeared to leave legendary works behind with the best materials they could get and matchless skills they had honed. Their works are treasures from traditional culture.

The four were indispensable to book readers' study and their progress involved active efforts from scholars. From their shape and decorative pattern to material chosen and making techniques, everything showed a scholarly taste in ancient times.

• 传统文房（现代）

书桌上摆放着各式传统文房用具，与墙上悬挂的书法、古朴的家具相得益彰。

Study in traditional style (contemporary product)

On the desk are traditional things needed in the study, which match perfectly with calligraphic works hanging on the wall and traditional-style furniture around.

笔
The Writing Brush

　　文房四宝中的"笔"是指"毛笔"。毛笔是中国古代先民所创造的书画工具，由兽毛捆缚于笔管制成。笔头柔软富有弹性，能够表现出汉字点、撇、横、捺的变化，以及中国山水画的浓淡起伏。毛笔位居文房四宝之首，其使用和普及是中国文化兴盛的标志。

One of the four treasures, the writing brush, an invention by distant ancestors, is made with hairs of an animal bound to the end of the brush holder. The hairs are soft and resilient, able to write different strokes of a Chinese character and paint dark or pale strokes Chinese landscape requiring. Always as the first one mentioned of the four, the writing brush with its popularity degree marked the progress of Chinese culture.

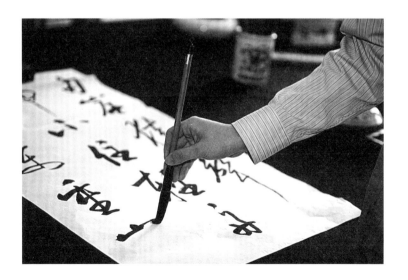

> 笔的历史

中国人使用毛笔的历史十分悠久，最原始的毛笔出现在距今10000～4000年的新石器时代，此后经过不断改良，至魏晋时期（220—581）方基本定型。唐代（618—907）之后，宣笔、湖笔的出现，是制笔工艺迅速发展的标志。明清时期（1368—1911），毛笔已成为文房中必不可少的工具，其造型、纹饰及工艺更加精湛。

毛笔的起源

关于毛笔起源于何时，至今尚无定论。历史上有"蒙恬造笔"的传说。蒙恬是秦朝名将，有"中华第一勇士"之誉，然而这位勇士却与毛笔的起源有着密切的联系。

相传蒙恬带兵在外作战，要定

> History of Writing Brush

Chinese nation has a long history of using writing brushes. The earliest ones appeared about something between 10 thousand and four thousand years ago during the Neolithic Age. Later, they experienced repeated innovations until the Wei and the Jin Dynasties (220-581) when their design was finalized. After the Tang Dynasty (618-907), the appearance of the famous *Xuan* and *Hu* styles marked a fast track that their making technology was on. By the Ming and the Qing Dynasties (1368-1911), writing brushes had become indispensable in any one's study and their design, decorative pattern and making technology reached a level never obtained before.

Origin of Writing Brush

It is still an open question as for the time

● 蒙恬塑像

蒙恬（？—前210），秦朝著名将领，因对毛笔的改良做出重大贡献而被人们尊奉为"笔祖"。

Meng Tian

Meng Tian (?-210 B.C.), a famous army general of the Qin Dynasty, was taken as the ancestor of writing brush because of a significant innovation he made on this writing tool.

期写战报呈送秦王，由于没有便利的书写工具，战报常常延期送到，为此蒙恬多次受罚。一天，蒙恬看见一只被箭射伤的兔子，它的尾巴在地上拖出了血迹，便有了灵感。他剪下一些兔尾毛，插在竹管上，试着用它来写字。他将兔毛做的笔往墨盘里一蘸，发现写起字竟然非

when the writing brush was invented, yet a legend ascribed it to Meng Tian, an army general of the Qin Dynasty (221 B.C.-206 B.C.) with unusual military exploits to his name. He was regarded as "number one warrior of the nation". Obviously he had something to do with the invention.

Each time he was out in battlefields, as the legend says, he was supposed to send reports about war progress to the Qin ruler at regular interval. Yet, duc to the lack of convenient writing tools his reports were often past due. Because of this Meng Tian was often reprimanded and even penalized. One day, after viewing a wounded rabbit leaving a trail of blood on the ground, he got an idea. He cut some hairs from the dead rabbit, which he tied to the end of a brush holder, with which he tried to pick up ink. Much to his excitement, it worked wonderfully. So he promoted this invention. This is why later generations have taken him as the inventor.

It's a legend after all. In fact, the appearance of the writing brush appeared much earlier than the Qin Dynasty (221 B.C.-206 B.C.). By unearthed objects pcople in the Neolithic Age already used something like a brush to write. The

常流畅。后来蒙恬将这种制笔工艺推广开来，人们因此将蒙恬视为制笔的始祖。

传说终归是传说，事实上，毛笔的出现远早于秦朝（前221—前206）。从出土文物提供的证据来看，最迟在新石器时代就有类似毛笔的工具产生了。在新石器时代遗址出土的一些彩陶上，有刻意描绘的纹饰图案。这些纹饰清晰流畅，显然不是质地坚硬的刻画工具所能完成的，而应是由柔软的类似毛笔的工具描绘而成。因此考古学家推断新石器时代就已经出现了毛笔的雏形。

decorative patterns appearing on the painted pottery unearthed in relic sites from this period of history have flowing lines elaborately drawn, obviously not by a hard-tip writing tool but something with a very soft tip, something just like the writing brush. According to archeologists, the Neolithic Age should be the time when the earliest form of the writing brush appeared.

• 供奉笔祖蒙恬尊像碑记
Stone inscription on the shrine for Meng Tian, inventor of writing brushes

新石器时代彩陶

　　新石器时代随着制陶工艺的成熟，在陶器器表或内壁进行彩绘的装饰手法逐渐流行起来。比较具有代表性的有黄河上游的马家窑文化（距今约5000～4000年）、黄河中游的仰韶文化（距今约7000～5000年），以及黄河下游的大汶口文化（距今约6000～4000年）等遗址中出土的一大批彩陶制品。这些陶器表面的纹饰大多以类似毛笔的工具绘制而成，黑色为主要基调，以几何纹饰为主，其他纹饰也大多以简单的线条为元素构成。

Painted Pottery During the Neolithic Age

With the maturity of pottery making in the Neolithic Age, decoration applied to outside and inside walls became popular. In this, representative works were found in Majiayao Culture (about 5000~4000 years ago) on the upper ranges of the Yellow River, the Yangshao Culture (about 7000~5000 years ago) on the middle ranges of the Yellow River and the Dawenkou Culture (about 6000~4000 years ago) on the lower ranges of the Yellow River. Many have black geometric shapes drawn by something like the writing brush very much. Some have simple lines only.

- 网格纹彩陶船形壶（仰韶文化）

  Pottery boat-shape pot with painted grids(Yangshao Culture, about 7000~5000 years ago)

- 豆荚纹彩陶钵（仰韶文化）

  Painted pottery bowl with bean pattern(Yangshao Culture, about 7000~5000 years ago)

- 鸟纹彩陶壶（马家窑文化）

  Pottery pot with a bird pattern(Majiayao Culture, about 5000~4000 years ago)

- 花叶纹小口彩陶壶（大汶口文化）

  Small-mouth pottery pot painted with flower patterns(Dawenkou Culture, about 6000~4000 years ago)

在河南安阳殷墟出土的甲骨片上也残留有朱书与墨迹，应为毛笔所书。所以，毛笔的起源是在殷商（前1600—前1046）之前，而不是秦朝蒙恬所创。1954年，在湖南省长沙市左家公山战国楚墓出土了一支毛笔，这是目前发现的最早的毛笔。1958年，在河南省信阳市长关台战国楚墓中也出土了一支竹杆毛笔，在制作结构和使用方法上都与左家公山战国楚墓出土的毛笔相似。

Characters in cinnabar and ink were also found in oracle bones unearthed in the Yin Dynasty ruins of Anyang, Henan Province, supposed to have been done by a writing brush. The Yin Dynasty, also called Shang (1600B.C.-1046 B.C.), was much earlier than Meng Tian's time and this proved beyond doubts the invention of the writing brush was not creditable to Meng Tian. In 1954, a writing brush in a real sense was discovered in Zuojiagong Mount of Changsha, Hunan Province, from a Chu tomb of the Warring States Period (475 B.C.-221 B.C.). That was the earliest writing brush ever found by now. In 1958, another writing brush with a bamboo holder was found in Changguantai, Xinyang of Henan Province, also from a Chu tomb. The two were very similar in structure and the way of use.

毛笔（战国）

这支毛笔是中国迄今发现最早的毛笔，被称为"战国笔"，又因其出土于楚墓而称为"楚笔"。笔头是用兔毛制成，笔杆是竹制的，笔头用丝缠绕绑扎成束包扎在笔杆的外侧，再封漆固定。

Writing brush (Warring States Period, 475 B.C.-221 B.C.)

This writing brush, the oldest ever found in China, is called "the writing brush from the Warring States Period" or "the Chu writing brush" from the tomb in which it was found. It had rabbit hairs and a bamboo holder. The hairs were fastened to one end before lacquer was applied to make it stronger.

"笔"字的演变
Changes in history on the character "writing brush"

林 → 甫 → 筆 → 笔

金文→篆书→繁体字→简体字

Bronze inscription—seal script—traditional character —simplified form

- 金文里（聿）字像彐（手）持丨（聿），篆书中则是在聿字上加了"竹"构成笔字。

The bronze inscription, a style from the inscriptions often found on ancient bronze objects, is a pictograph resembling a hand holding something, while the seal script has the word "bamboo" in it to complete the meaning "writing brush".

笔
The Writing Brush

秦汉时期的毛笔

秦代（前221—前206）以前，毛笔多以枯木为笔杆，到秦代才开始以竹为笔杆。秦始皇统一六国后，在文化方面统一了文字，实行"书同文"，规定"篆书"为统一字体，毛笔的使用也由此推广至全国。此时，毛笔形成了竹管、兽毫合成的基本形制，有些地方已经开始因制作毛笔而著称。另外，秦代已经出现用细竹管制成的中部镂空的笔管套，用以保护毛笔，可见当

Writing Brushes Made During the Qin and the Han Dynasties

Before the Qin Dynasty (221B.C.-206 B.C.), most writing brushes had holders from weathered wood. Bamboo ones replaced the wood during the Qin Dynasty. After Qin Shi Huang, the first emperor of Qin who unified China and promoted a unified written language that took the Seal characters as the only style permissible to use, the use of writing brush became nationwide practice. By then, the structure of writing brush had

时制笔工艺的完善程度。

汉代（前206—公元220）时，毛笔的制造工艺得到了进一步的发展。笔头除了用兔毛、羊毛外，还出现了将狼毛、鹿毛、狸毛混合制成的"兼毫笔"。兼毫笔的笔头多以兔毫为笔柱，羊毛裹在兔毫的外面，使毛笔的特性因混合比例不同而形成差异，满足了不同书写者的需要。笔管的质地和装饰在汉代也逐渐引起人们的注意，据文献记载，当时的笔管已有"雕以黄金，饰以和璧，缀以隋珠，文以翡翠"的情况，十分华丽。

汉代还有一种"簪白笔"，是一种笔管长约20厘米，笔尾部削成尖形，并髹之以漆的毛笔。

taken shape, a bamboo holder with a tip of animal hairs. Some places made fame out of their making. About this time, the writing brush cap as protection appeared in the form of a hollow bamboo tube.

Further progress was made during the Han Dynasty (206 B.C.-220 A.D.). Apart from rabbit or goat hairs, hairs from other animals like weasel, deer and leopard cat were used together, called *jian hao*, for a better performance. Usually, *jian hao* had rabbit hairs in the middle and goat hairs around, with different percentages to satisfy different needs. Penholders' material and decoration began to draw attention. By history records, some writing brushes made then had gold, jade, pearl and emerald as decoration.

A new variety appeared in the Han Dynasty, *Zanbai* (literally, hairpin white) writing brush, 20 centimeters long on the holder pointed at one end and coated with lacquer.

• 狼毫笔（汉）
Writing brush with weasel hairs
(Han Dynasty, 206B.C.-220A.D.)

竹杆羊毫笔（秦）

1975年在湖北省云梦睡虎地秦墓中出土了三支以竹为管的毛笔，这是其中一支。竹管的前端被凿出孔，笔头嵌入其中。

Writing brush made with bamboo and goat hairs (Qin Dynasty, 221B.C.-206B.C.)

Three writing brushes with bamboo holders were discovered from a Qin-dynasty tomb in 1975 in Hubei Province. This is one of the three, whose end is hollowed to receive brush hairs.

簪白笔

汉代文官奏事，常用毛笔将所奏之事写在笏（古代官员上朝时拿着的手板，多由竹片制成）上，写完之后即将毛笔插在发髻或帽子上。后来这种做法逐渐演变成一种官服制度，凡文官上朝，皆须插笔，笔尖不蘸墨汁，纯粹用作装饰，称"簪白笔"制度。

Zanbai Writing Brush

Civil officials during the Han Dynasty appeared before the throne with a memo written on a bamboo slip they held in hand and a writing brush either on their hair or headwear. This practice progressed into a fashion. Every civil official appeared in court wore a writing brush, with no ink on its tip as a hairpin just for decoration purpose.

簪
Zan (hairpin)

笏
Hu (bamboo hand board)

- 汉代文官像
Civil official of the Han Dynasty

魏晋南北朝时期的毛笔

　　魏晋南北朝时期（220—589），毛笔的发展不仅没有受到社会动荡的影响，而且形成了新的特点。这一时期，人们习惯跪坐在矮儿前悬肘书写，为了便于书写，笔杆的部分逐渐变短，笔锋的弹性得到加强，以"鼠须笔"、"紫毫笔"为代表的短杆笔深受文人的喜爱。中国书法史上的名作《兰亭序》便是"书圣"王羲之用"鼠须笔"（松鼠的尾毫所制）所作。

Writing Brushes Made During the Wei, the Jin and the Southern and Northern Dynasties

During the period of these dynasties (220-589) writing brush making continued to progress in spite of social turbulences. People on knees wrote on a low desk with wrist never touching it. For convenience writing brushes made in this time became shorter on the holder but more elastic on tip. Popular styles were squirrel tail hairs and dark hairs from mountain rabbits, very much favored by scholars. With a brush of the former style calligraphy sage Wang Xizhi did his immortal work in Chinese history, *Lan Ting Xu* or *The Preface to the Collection of Writings in Lanting*.

● 矮几（现代）
矮几的四足较短，书写时需跪坐在前。
Low desk(contemporary product)
Because of its short legs, one had to write on knees on a desk like this.

王羲之与《兰亭序》

　　王羲之（303—361，一作321—379），字逸少，祖籍琅琊临沂（今属山东省），后迁会稽（今浙江省绍兴市），中国东晋书法家，有"书圣"之称。他出身名门望族，其家族曾助东晋建朝于建康（今江苏省南京市）。王羲之曾官至右军将军，会稽内史，人称"王右军"、"王会稽"。世人对王羲之印象最深的是他的书法，他善隶、草、楷、行等各种字体的书法，而他的名作《兰亭序》被誉为"天下第一行书"，为历代书法家所推崇。

● 王羲之像
Wang Xizhi

Wang Xizhi and his *Lan Ting Xu*

Wang Xizhi (303-361 or 321-379), calligraphy sage in the Eastern Jin Dynasty, styled himself as Yishao, came from Linyi in present-day Shandong Province but later moved to Kuaiji, today's Shaoxing in Zhejiang Province. Because he once served in the army as a general, he was also called with respect "Right General Wang" or "Wang Kuaiji". As a great master in all styles of writing his calligraphy was legendary. *Lan Ting Xu* was an immortal work in running script admired throughout history.

● 《兰亭序》【局部】王羲之（晋）

　　《兰亭序》作于东晋穆帝永和九年（353）。当时王羲之与谢安、孙绰等41人，会于山阴（今浙江绍兴）兰亭，众人作了几十首诗汇集起来，公推德高望重的王羲之写一序文，记录这次雅集。王羲之在酒兴之下，用鼠须笔写下了二十八行、三百二十四字，被后人誉为"天下第一行书"的《兰亭序》。

Lan Ting Xu (detail), by Wang Xizhi (Jin Dynasty, 265-420)

This calligraphic work was done in 353, the ninth year of Yonghe Reign of Emperor Mu of the Eastern Jin Dynasty on a drinking party with 41 friends in Shanyin (present-day Shaoxing, Zhejiang Province). They composed poems over wine. Wang Xizhi was asked to write a foreword for the collection of these poems, which he did in a tipsy condition with a writing brush of squirrel tail hairs. This was how this immortal work, described as the best calligraphic piece in running script made in any time and in any place, 324 characters in 28 lines, was born.

魏晋南北朝时期，毛笔的制作受到当时奢侈之风的影响，笔管的材质出现了金银、象牙、犀角、玉石等名贵材料，有的笔管上还雕刻有精美的图案作为装饰。《太平广记》中就记载有梁元帝曾有金、银、竹三管笔，分别用于记录不同品行、地位之人的事迹：忠孝两全者以金管笔书写；德行高尚者以银管笔书写；文章华丽者以斑竹笔书写。

Due to a craze for luxury among the rich and powerful during the Wei, the Jin and the Southern and Northern Dynasties, materials for penholder also took a turn for expensive materials like gold, silver, ivory, rhinoceros horn or jade, some having elaborate decoration to go with. By *Tai Ping Guang Ji* or *The Encyclopedia of Peace and Tranquility* Emperor Yuan of the Liang Dynasty had three writing brushes he loved most, gold, silver and bamboo, to record the conducts of his ministers: the gold for those loyal to him and pious to their parents, the silver for those of virtues and the bamboo for writers in a flowery style.

• 梁元帝的金、银、竹笔（南朝）
从左到右依次为银笔、金笔、竹笔。
The gold, silver and bamboo writing brushes Emperor Yuan of the Liang Dynasty used (the Southern Dynasty, 420-589)
The silver, gold and the bamboo writing brushes (from left to right)

江淹梦笔

　　江淹，南朝文学家。传说他小时候曾经梦见一位老先生送给他一支五色笔，此后，他的诗文就非常出色。后来，他又梦见五色笔被那位先生索回，原本才思敏捷的江淹则文思枯竭，人们评价他为"江郎才尽"。

　　"江淹梦笔"的典故中将毛笔作为评断勤学苦练的指标，也是才思的代表。典故中的江淹可以因为梦到毛笔而文思泉涌，因为梦见失笔而才尽，可见毛笔在文人心目中是多么重要。

Jiang Yan Receiving Brush In Dream

Jiang Yan, a man of letters during the Southern Dynasty, once had a dream in which he received a five-color writing brushfrom someone. With the pen, as the legend says, he was able to write excellent articles to surprise everyone. Later, also in his dream, the pen was taken back by the man who had given it to him and from this time on his literary talent was no more. So came the popular saying "The imaginative power for writing is gone" for someone whose inspiration had dried up.

　　In this story, the writing brush was personified as the logo of hard work and talent. With it, Jiang Yan was able to write marvelous writings and without it he had no inspiration left. What is the importance of a writing brush to a man of letters? This story tells.

● 杭州"邵芝岩"笔庄的湖笔
Hu style brushes, from Shaozhiyan in Hangzhou

隋唐时期的毛笔

隋唐时期（581—907）是毛笔发展的一个重要时期，出现了第一个制笔中心——宣州（今安徽省宣城市），著名的"宣笔"即产于此地。宣笔在选材、制作、性能上都超过了前代，其笔头坚挺，满足了当时人们席地而坐的书写需求。宣笔在隋唐时期风行一时，唐代朝廷用笔多为宣州所制。

Writing Brushes Made During the Sui and the Tang Dynasties

These two dynasties (581-907) saw a fast progress in writing brush making. Xuanzhou (present-day Xuancheng of Anhui Province) appeared as the first center for brush making business China ever had in history. The writing brush made in this place was affectionately called "*Xuan*-style Writing Brush" for its better material and better making technology than those in previous dynasties. The hairs became harder, very nice for writing when sitting on floor. Instantly, the use of *Xuan* style writing brush became a vogue during the Sui and Tang Dynasties. Inside the Tang court, *Xuan* brushes, nothing else, were used.

宣笔

宣笔又名"徽笔"，是中国古代著名的书画笔。宣州自秦代时已有制笔业，宣笔见于正史始于汉代。东晋时期（317—420），宣州陈氏是著名的制笔世家，其用山兔毛制成的一种紫毫毛笔，笔锋坚挺耐用，易于书写，但产量不高故很难买到。大书法家王羲之都曾向陈氏求笔。唐代（618—907）时，宣州成为全国的制笔中心。当时大江南北都有专门的制笔作坊，出现了诸葛氏、吕道人、汪伯力等制笔名家，宣笔发展到天下独尊的地位，一直到元代时才被后起的湖笔所取代。

The *Xuan* Style Writing Brushes

The *Xuan* style writing brush, also called the *Hui* style brush, was famous for writing and painting in ancient China. Back to the Qin Dynasty writing brush making appeared in Xuanzhou. The earliest official documentation of brush making happened in the Han Dynasty. Later, during the Eastern Jin Dynasty, Xuanzhou had its famous family business in this trade, the Chen Family. The brushes it made with dark hairs from mountain rabbits were unable to meet the huge market need. Even the calligraphy sage Wang Xizhi begged for one. Later, during the Tang Dynasty (618-907), Xuanzhou became the center of this trade in the country. Family businesses mushroomed along the Yangtze with big names like Zhuge, Lv Daoren and Wang Boli. *Xuan* style writing brushes dominated the market until the Yuan Dynasty (1279-1368) when writing brushes from Huzhou rose to take away the glory.

柳公权像

柳公权（778—865），字诚悬，唐代著名书法家。他善写楷书，与当时另一位书法家颜真卿齐名。

Liu Gongquan

Liu Gongquan (778-865), alias Chengxuan, famous calligrapher in the Tang Dynasty. His strong hand was the regular script and he enjoyed the same prestige as another calligraphy artist, his contemporary Yan Zhenqing.

《金刚经》【局部】柳公权（唐）

Vajracchedika-sutra (detail), by Liu Gongquan (Tang Dynasty, 618-907)

● **宣笔（现代）**

Xuan style writing brushes (contemporary product)

宣笔以选料严格、精工细作著称，具有毛纯耐用、刚柔适中、尖圆齐健"四德"兼全的独特风格。

Xuan style brushes are famous for their tough material selection and painstaking technology in making. The hairs they use are endurable, soft and vigorous, able to meet all the requirements for a nice brush.

　　隋唐时期制笔沿用魏晋时期的方法，制造锋短、形如鸡距的"鸡距笔"。后来因其吸墨性不好且易干枯，制笔工匠又改进制造出锋长柔软、吸墨性好的长锋笔。长锋笔书写流畅，适合行草书写，它的出现成就了以张旭、怀素为代表的草书大家，为唐宋书法带来了纵横洒脱的新风。

Writing brushes made during the Sui and the Tang Dynasties followed the way of previous the Wei and the Jin Dynasties, having short brush tips. Later, this short tip style was abandoned simply because it picked little ink and it dried up easily. They were replaced by soft long-hair brush tips much better in absorbing ink for continuous writing, perfect for running and cursive script writing. This progress enabled calligraphic giants to appear like Zhang Xu and Huai Su. Together, they brought a brand new look to the Tang-dynasty calligraphic art.

● 鸡距笔（唐）

鸡距笔因其形制似鸡爪后面的距而得名，其特点是笔锋短小犀利，缺点是吸墨性不好，易干枯。

Cockspur writing brush (Tang Dynasty, 618-907)

Because of a shape very much like cockspur it got this name. It featured a small and short tip that picked up little ink but dried up easily.

● 《自叙帖》【局部】怀素（唐）

《自叙帖》成书于唐大历十二（777）年，是唐代草书大家怀素的经典之作。全卷强调连绵之势，长锋笔的使用是此佳作的重要基础。

My Narration (detail), calligraphic work by Huai Su (Tang Dynasty, 618-907)

This piece, done in 777, the 12th year of Dali Reign of Tang, was the best calligraphic work Huai Su ever did. Its flowing writing seemed never broken. The long hair writing brush made this possible.

李白"梦笔生花"

李白（701—762），唐朝著名诗人，有"诗仙"之称。

相传，李白在少年时代曾经做过一个奇特的梦。梦中，他在奋笔疾书，突然发现笔头上开出一朵洁白如玉的莲花来，光彩夺目，正在诧异之间，一张张白纸又从天而至，落到他的眼前。从此以后，李白的才思更加锐进，创作了大量的不朽诗篇，成为举世闻名的大诗人。后来，"梦笔生花"一词被用来形容文人文笔优美、风格俊逸。

"Writing Brush Blooms" in Li Bai's Dream

Li Bai (701-762) was the legendary poet of the Tang Dynasty.

He had a very strange dream in his boyhood, as the legend says. While he was writing he suddenly saw a brilliant bloom coming from the end of his brush. While he was confused sheets of white paper fell from the sky to land around him. From this moment on, his literary talents doubled, leaving one immortal poem after another and he was viewed as unchallengeable in attainments. This story was later boiled down to a proverb to describe a graceful style in which one writes.

● 李白像
Li Bai

● 北京戴月轩精制湖笔
Hu style writing brush, from Dai Yue Xuan, Beijing

宋元时期的毛笔

宋元时期（960—1368），毛笔的制作更加发达，在种类和制笔工艺上都超越唐代。北宋时期（960—1127），宣州仍然是当时的制笔中心，但到了北宋后期，为了逃避战乱，宣州的许多制笔名匠逃至湖州（今属浙江省），促进了湖州毛笔制造工艺的发展。南宋（1127—1279）迁都杭州，其政治、经济、文化中心也都逐渐转移至江南地区。到元代（1271—1368）时，湖州成为继宣州之后的第二个毛笔制造中心，"湖笔"从此名扬天下，并成为御用笔。

• 竹管笔（宋）
Bamboo holder writing brushes (Song Dynasty, 960-1279)

Writing Brushes Made During the Song and the Yuan Dynasties

Writing brush making progressed even faster during the Song and the Yuan Dynasties (960-1368), with more brush varieties than those of the previous Tang Dynasty. In its first half, commonly called the Northern Song (960-1127), Xuanzhou was still a center of this trade. But at the end of the Northern Song, many highly skilled makers escaped from wars to Huzhou of present-day Zhejiang Province and this gave birth to writing brush making in Huzhou. With the relocation of the capital city by the Southern Song (1127-1279) government to Hangzhou, political, economic and cultural center of the nation shifted to China's south. By the Yuan Dynasty (1271-1368) that followed Song Huzhou had succeeded Xuanzhou as the center in the country for writing brush making business. The fame of the brushes made there, commonly called the *Hu* style brush, became widely known. Emperors used the *Hu* style brush only.

冯应科、陆文宝制笔

冯应科和陆文宝是元代毛笔制造名匠，两个人并称为"冯陆"。据文献记载，冯应科制的笔妙绝天下，经常被列为贡品，与赵子昂的字、钱舜举的画合称为"吴兴三绝"。

Brushes Made by Feng Yingke and Lu Wenbao

Both enjoyed a big name during the Yuan Dynasty, often mentioned together as "Feng and Lu". By history books Feng's products were made exclusively for emperor's use. The brush he made, together with the calligraphic works by Zhao Ziang and paintings by Qian Shunju, were described as "three wonders" from Wuxing.

- 冯应科像
  Feng Yingke

- 冯应科制笔（元）
  The writing brush made by Feng Yingke (Yuan Dynasty, 1271-1368)

- 陆文宝制笔（元）
  The writing brush made by Lu Wenbao (Yuan Dynasty, 1271-1368)

湖笔

湖笔的制作以羊毫为主，紫毫、狼毫并用。湖笔按性能可划分为软毫、硬毫、兼毫三种，可满足不同的书写需要。硬毫笔弹性好，笔力强，落墨劲；软毫笔含墨饱满，易于挥洒；兼毫笔刚柔并济，易于掌控。

湖笔之所以在元代时得到迅速发展，与当时文人的参与有很大的关系。元代著名的书画家赵孟頫是湖州人氏，他不仅在书法、绘画方面取得了极高的成就，在制笔方面也颇有造诣。他从小就和笔工相熟，并留意制笔技艺，多方搜集前辈笔匠的秘技妙诀，潜心研究，还将自己的制笔感悟告诉好友陆文宝，后来陆文宝成为当时制笔的名家。

The *Hu* Style Writing Brush

Most *Hu* style writing brushes took goat, rabbit and weasel hairs as materials and used them together. They had different degrees in hardness to satisfy different needs—soft, hard and medium. Brushes with hard tips featured elasticity and wrote vigorous brushstrokes; brushes with soft tips picked up more ink than other kinds and were good for continuous writing; while brushes made with more varieties of hairs than one had advantages of both and were more controllable.

Why did the *Hu* style writing brush gain a rapid progress during the Yuan Dynasty? Because of an active involvement from men of letters. Zhao Mengfu, a famous artist in paining and calligraphy, was a Huzhou native. He was also a skilled brush maker because when he was very young he had hung around skillful makers and collected tips from them. Later, he passed his experience on to one of his friends, Lu Wenbao, who later developed into a renowned master maker.

- **赵孟頫像**

赵孟頫（1254—1322），字子昂，吴兴（今浙江省湖州市）人，元代著名书画家。赵孟頫博学多才，能诗善文，精通诗文、绘画、乐律，尤以书法和绘画成就最高，与颜真卿、柳公权、欧阳询并称为"楷书四大家"。

Zhao Mengfu

Zhao Mengfu (1254-1322), alias Ziang, a native of Wuxing (present-day Huzhou of Zhejiang Province), famous artist in painting and calligraphy, a great talent in academic learning, poetry composing and essay writing, even in music. But the highest attainments he achieved were in painting and calligraphy, and this left him standing shoulder to shoulder with Yan Zhenqing, Liu Gongquan and Ouyang Xun as "the great four calligraphers in regular script".

- 《洛神赋》【局部】赵孟頫（元）

For the Goddess of Luo (detail), by Zhao Mengfu (Yuan Dynasty, 1271-1368)

这一时期，人们逐渐告别了跪坐的书写方式，改为坐在椅子上伏案悬腕书写，因此要求毛笔笔杆较短、笔锋硬中有软。在笔毛的选料上，除了传统的兔毫外，狼毫、羊毫应用越来越多，鼠尾毫、鸡毫等也有使用。在制笔工艺上，笔匠们制造出更加软熟、虚锋、散毫的新式毛笔"散卓笔"，笔毛中心有物的"枣心笔"，以及"丁香笔"等。

Beginning from this period of history people no longer wrote in a kneeling position but seated when writing, still keeping wrist from touching the desk. And this required a short brush holder and a tip medium hard. Materials, apart from the traditional rabbit hairs, became diversified to include hairs from weasels and goats, squirrel tail hairs and even chicken feathers. Brush makers developed new types called *Sanzhuo*, *Zaoxin* and *Dingxiang* (lilac). All had new properties and a better performance. *Zaoxin* even had something hard in the middle of the tip.

• 竹管鸡毫笔（宋）
Writing brush with bamboo holder and chicken feathers (Song Dynasty, 960-1279)

丁香笔

丁香笔是宋代的一种名笔，以精选的紫毫为柱芯，羊毫为副，以制笔名家张遇制作的最为著名。大书法家黄庭坚评价其"捻心极圆，束颉有力"。丁香笔自张遇之后就鲜见于世，其制法现已失传。

Lilac Writing Brush

A very famous variety during the Song Dynasty, this lilac brush had dark hairs from hares for the major part of the tip and goat's hairs as a supplement. Among all, Zhang Yu was best known for this variety. To great calligrapher Huang Tingjian, this variety had unusual properties other varieties didn't have and was able to do brushstrokes other varieties couldn't. Yet lilac products were very rare and their making technology got lost.

● 丁香笔选用的精品紫毫
Best dark hairs for a lilac brush.

明清时期的毛笔

Writing Brushes Made During the Ming and the Qing Dynasties

明清时期（1368—1911），毛笔的制造仍以湖州为中心，逐渐发展到杭州、绍兴等地。各大城市都出现了笔庄，专门销售毛笔，这些笔庄往往会挂上"湖笔"或"宣笔"的牌子。由于明清时期

The Ming and the Qing Dynasties (1368-1911) still had Huzhou as the center for writing brush making business. The business had spread to nearby Hangzhou and Shaoxing. In many cities, shops in writing brush business appeared and most

书画艺术繁荣，更加促进了制笔业的发展，毛笔的制作工艺也达到了鼎盛。

● "大明万历"款五彩龙凤笔（明）

Five-color dragon and phoenix writing brush, a royal style during the Wanli Reign (Ming Dynasty, 1368-1644)

明清两代毛笔的制作受到御用笔和官府用笔追求奢华风格的影响，注重材料的选择和装饰的效果，风格较为华丽，具有浓厚的艺术韵味。从笔头的选毫来看，皇室和官府大多选用貂毫、熊毫等珍贵的动物毛；从笔杆的质地来看，除常用的竹木管外，还有用金、银、瓷、象牙、雕漆、玳瑁等制成的笔

of them proudly had a *Hu* or *Xuan* style writing brush signboard outside. Due to the then booming business in painting and calligraphy, writing brush making was on a fast development track and the technique up onto a higher level never obtained before.

Because of the orders placed by the royal family and government, writing brushes made during the Ming and the Qing Dynasties had a glaring pursuit for luxury. Makers spared no effort and cost for the best material available and the most eye-catching decoration to go with. Most tips of the brushes for the royal use had expensive marten or bear hairs. Apart from bamboo, the traditional material for brush holders, gold, silver, porcelain, ivory, lacquer, even hawksbill were used. The decoration on the holder and the cap was very eye-catching, with impressive carvings or precious things inlaid. The most expensive types included the black lacquer inlaid, carved lacquer, sandalwood, blue and white porcelain and famille-rose china.

More varieties never seen before appeared during the Ming and Qing Dynasties for different needs in painting and calligraphy, under the names of *Dou Bi*, *Zhua Bi*, *Ti Bi* and *Lian Bi*, etc. Brush

管；从笔杆的装饰来看，其雕刻和镶嵌异常精美，有黑彩漆镶嵌笔管、剔红笔管、檀香木雕笔管、青花瓷笔管、粉彩瓷笔管等装饰精美的笔管。

tips also had more varieties, the bamboo shoot, *Xiangpan*, orchid and gourd styles being some.

• 牛筋驼毛笔（明）
Cowheel writing brush with camel hairs (Ming Dynasty, 1368-1644)

• 木、玉、牙、角制
笔管的笔（清）
Writing brushes made with wood, jade, ivory and rhino horn (Qing Dynasty, 1644-1911)

此外，明清时期毛笔的品种更加丰富。制笔工匠根据书法、绘画的具体需要，创造出了斗笔、抓笔、提笔、联笔等新品种。在笔头的部分，捆扎出竹笋式、香盘式、兰花式、葫芦式等多种形式。

• 紫檀木嵌银丝大抓笔（清）
Narra holding brushes inlaid with silver threads (Qing Dynasty, 1644-1911)

毛笔的制作流程
Steps to Make Writing Brushes

　　毛笔看似简单，但其制作过程却十分复杂，从选料到成笔要经过百余道工序。古代毛笔制作中最主要的工序有以下几个：

Seemingly simple, the steps were actually very complicated and demanding. From the material choosing to the final finishing there were a hundred steps, but the major ones being the following few:

　　选毫：将采集的动物毛全都放在砧板上，将无用的杂毛去除，收集剩余的毫毛。选毫是制笔成败的关键，因此要求极其严格，有"千万毛中选一毫"之说。选好的毫毛还要按照粗细、长短、软硬度进行分类，以满足制笔的不同需要。

　　Hairs Chosen: The selected animal hairs were left on board for further sorting; only the best ones were used. This step was crucial because it determined success or failure for the final product. "Using only the best of the best" was not an exaggeration for this step. Even those selected were sorted again by their thickness, length and degrees of hardness used for different varieties.

● 制笔的各种笔毛
Hairs chosen for tips

　　熟毫：将毫毛按类别浸泡在石灰水中，然后去脂、去腥，经过这种处理的笔毫有的毛色偏黄，有的发白，弹性增强，经久耐用。

　　"Cooking" the Hairs: "Cooking" meant to leave the hairs selected inside limestone water to remove grease and bad odor. After "cooking" hairs took on a yellowish or cream look but became more elastic and endurable.

● 熟毫
"Cooking" the hairs

水作工：是毛笔制作中最关键的工序之一。将熟毫放在水盆内用牛角梳反复洗涤梳理，然后将毫毛制成片状，放在兽骨或压力板上反复地按压拉扯，使所有毫毛都整齐平铺于板面上，再按照所需笔锋的长度截取毫毛，其要求是"顶峰毫齐"、"锋颖齐"、"下根齐"，而且要求清洁干净，这样便制成了半成品的笔头。

Processing with Water: This was also a crucial step. "Cooked" hairs were washed and combed repeatedly in water with an ox horn comb before they were pressed into very thin and flat pieces on a board. Then different lengths were picked out by needs. This was a very demanding step for every hair had to show very clean-cut ends and sides and free of dirt. By now, they were half-finished tips.

• 水作工
Processing with water

结头：这道工序是将制好的半成品笔头结扎。将处理好的笔毫晾干，按照比例搭配好后，用线将笔头扎紧缚牢。捆扎时用力要均匀，以防笔头变形。

Tip Making: This step was to tie the half finished hairs into a tip after they were complete dry and sorted by a prescribed percentage. Thread was used, and the force applied when tying had to be even, neither too hard nor too gentle. Otherwise, the tip might deform.

• 结头
Tip making

蒲墩：是指笔管的选用和制作。笔管的材料以直、坚实、光滑润洁者为好。选好的管料经加工后，将两端挫平，再在一端挖出与笔头相配的笔斗，以装填笔头。

Pu Dun: *Pu Dun* means selecting of materials and making the holder. Materials chosen had to be very straight, hard and smooth and even better, shining. After initial processing the material was filed away on both ends. One end was hollowed to receive the tip.

装套：将制好的笔头和笔管进行装配，如有笔帽也包括在内。将笔头的底部放于火上烤热，并均匀地滴上热松香，使其渗入到笔毫的内部，这样毫毛才不易脱落，笔锋也更加锋利。

Capping: This meant to assemble the tip and the holder and a cap if there was one. The end of the tip was heated first on fire before receiving melted rosin until it went all the way down to depth. This was to fasten hairs and make the tip edge sharp.

择笔：将笔毫捻成笔头的形状，剔掉弯曲的毫毛，将笔头抹光，达到毛笔"尖、齐、圆、健"的要求。

Tip Shaping: This step was to twirl the hairs until they adopted the right shape. Less straight hairs were removed while smoothing until the tip met every one of the requirements: pointed, neat, round and vigorous.

雕刻：在笔管上雕刻笔名、古诗词、工匠名字等，明清时还有在笔管上雕刻图画的。

Carving: This step was to inscribe lines from a poem or the maker's name onto the holder. During the Ming and Qing Dynasties, a miniature painting was also seen.

● 择笔
Tip shaping

● 雕刻
Carving

> 毛笔的种类

　　毛笔的种类繁多，且有多种分类方法。比较常用的有按笔毫软硬、笔锋长短、笔头用途不同等来进行划分。

> Varieties of Writing Brushes

Writing brushes were in many varieties and the ways to classify were equally many. Very often the classification went by the hardness, length and function of tips and the needs they were made for.

● 胎发笔（清）

胎发笔是用新生婴儿第一次理发剃下的头发制成的毛笔。胎发细腻柔软，中国古代书香门第很多都将胎儿的毛发制成毛笔进行收藏，以此作为书香传世的表征。

Fetal-hair writing brush (Qing Dynasty, 1644-1911)

Fetal hair came from the first haircut an infant had. These hairs were exceptionally soft and tender. Since ancient times scholar's families collected these hairs for brush making as a symbol of age-old book-reading family.

毛笔的结构
Structure of a Writing Brush

毛笔在结构上分为笔头、笔管、笔帽三部分。其中以笔头最为重要，笔管装饰性最强，笔帽则属附件。

Structurally, a writing brush had three parts, the tip, the holder and the cap. Of the three, the tip was the most important while the holder the most decorative and the cap, just an accessory.

笔头，是毛笔蓄墨和写字的部分，常用兽毛制成。笔头从上至下可分为笔根、笔腰、笔锋、笔端四部分，从里至外又可分为芯毫、披毫和副毫三部分。

The tip was for keeping ink and doing brushstrokes. Most of the tips were made with animal hairs. From top to the bottom, the tip had four parts: the root, waist, edge and end. If from inside to the outside, it had three parts: *Xin Hao* (the core), *Pi Hao* (the outside hairs) and *Fu Hao* (the hairs in between).

芯毫：笔毫最内层的毫毛。
Xin Hao: the hairs at the core

副毫：芯毫与被毫中间的毫毛。
Fu Hao: the hairs in between

披毫：笔毫最外层的毫毛。
Pi Hao: the outside hairs

笔根：笔头插入笔管内的部分。
The root of the tip: the part inside the holder

笔腰：笔头与笔管接口到中间鼓腹的部分。
The waist: the part from the connection with the holder to the biggest width it had

笔锋：鼓腹以下到尖头的部分。
The edge: the part below the biggest width to the end

笔端：笔锋的最尖端。
The end: the farthest part of the tip

● 笔头结构
Structure of the writing brush tip

笔管，也称"笔杆"，是手握书写的部分。笔管的一端是装连笔头的笔斗，另一端是笔顶。笔顶的样式丰富，有的呈球形便于手握，有的呈横截面状，上面有挂头便于悬挂。

The holder was the part for the writer to hold. One end was hollow to receive hairs while the other end was often shaped into, say a ball for easy holding, or a cross section with a hook for convenient hanging.

• 笔管
Writing brush holder

笔帽又称"笔套"，是用来保护笔头不受损伤的工具。笔帽以竹质为多，也有木质或金属质的，现代笔帽则以塑料制品居多。

The writing brush cap was for a protection purpose, which was made with bamboo, some with wood and metal. Contemporary products are often plastic.

笔帽
brush cap

• **剔红人物狼毫笔（明）**
剔红，又名"雕红漆"，是在器物的胎体上刷上几十层甚至一两百层的红漆，等累积到一定的厚度时描上画稿，然后再雕刻出花纹。

Weasel-hair writing brush with human figure carved on lacquer (Ming Dynasty, 1368-1644)
Carved lacquer had another name, "red lacquer", which came from the way of its making: applying one hundred, even two hundred coats to the brush until the thickness was right to receive a draft before carving began.

根据笔毫软硬的不同，毛笔可分为硬毫笔、软毫笔、兼毫笔三种。

硬毫笔通常是用一种弹性较好、毛质较硬的兽毛来制作，常见的有狼毫、紫毫、鼠尾毫、鹿毫、马毫、猪毫、貂毫等。硬毫笔适宜

By different degrees of hardness, writing brushes could be categorized into three varieties: the hard, the soft and the medium that had hairs of different kinds.

The hard ones were more elastic, often made with tough animal hairs from

书写行书、草书，其特点是锋毫刚硬，弹性十足，落纸锋芒显露，枯湿燥润变化分明，写、绘出的线条刚劲挺拔，呈现瘦劲、锐利、峻峭之感。其不足之处是吸水性不强。

weasels, hares, goats, squirrel tail, deer, horses, hogs and martens. This variety was nice for running and cursive script writing, able to show vigor needed and a nice variation between wetness and dryness on paper. The brushstrokes it did might look tall and straight, thin and vigorous, sharp and steep. But this variety had a disadvantage: it picked up less ink than other kinds.

• **紫毫笔（元）**

紫毫笔即兔毫笔，是由野兔背脊上的一小撮毛制成，因毛色呈紫黑而得名。笔毫尖锐刚硬，毫毛直顺。因受兔毛长度的限制，只能作小笔，缺点是不耐久用，容易秃头。

Writing brushes with dark hairs from hare (Yuan Dynasty, 1271-1368)

The name of this variety came from the dark hairs from hares back. These hairs were hard, strong and straight but due to their less desirable length only fit for smaller brushes. Tips of hare hairs also had the disadvantage of being less durable and easily coming off.

软毫笔通常是用弹性较弱、毛质偏软的兽毛来制作，常用的软毫笔有羊毫笔、鸡毫笔、胎发笔、茅草笔等。软毫笔柔软灵活，富于变化，因此常用来书写篆书、隶书、行书或行草。软毫笔的特点是笔质

Soft-hair writing brushes had less elastic but soft animal hairs coming from goats, chicken, fetal hairs or thatch grass. This variety, as its name suggested, had soft tips that could easily change shape, thus very good for seal, official, running

柔软，吸水性强，着纸润腻，使用时婉转、圆润、灵活，锋毫便于铺开，写出的字笔画丰满。由于其弹性不足，多用于书法和水墨画的大片渲染。

and cursive script writing. It also featured a nice hydroscopic ability to leave very fine and well-round ink strokes on paper. However, due to less elasticity it was used more in calligraphy and ink and wash painting than regular writing.

· 山羊毛
Goat wool

· 羊毫笔（清）
羊毫笔以上等山羊毛制成，多用青、黄、黑、白色的羊毛。羊毫质地柔软，吸墨性好，适于制作较大的毛笔和长锋笔。

Goat-hair writing brushes (Qing Dynasty, 1644-1911)
Most goat-hair brushes took good-quality goat wool as the material in different colors: pale blue, yellow, black and white. The hairs were soft and good at absorbing ink, ideal for brushes of larger size or longer tips.

· 狼毫
Weasel-hair

· 狼毫笔（现代）
狼毫笔是用黄鼠狼的毫毛所制，是最常见的硬毫笔。笔毫富有弹性，笔头有光泽，但毛质较脆，不耐磨损。

Weasel-hair writing brush (contemporary product)
Most writing brushes of this variety had hard hairs from yellow weasels, which were elastic and glossy but crispy and less endurable.

兼毫笔是一种混合毫毛笔，是选用两种或两种以上软硬不同的毫毛按照一定的比例组合而制成。兼毫笔将硬毫笔的弹性和软毫笔的吸水性完美地统一起来，可以满足书写多种字体或绘画的要求，运用十分广泛。最常见的兼毫笔有紫羊毫笔（紫毫为芯、羊毫为披）、紫狼毫笔（紫毫为芯、狼毫为披）和白云笔（狼毫为芯、羊毫为披）三种。

Writing brushes with mixed hairs made another variety under the name of *Jian Hao*, which took hairs of different hardness by a certain ratio. This variety was meant to pick up the advantages of other kinds to satisfy a much wider range of needs. The most common kinds in this variety were three: *Zi Yang Hao* with hare hairs at the core and goat hairs around; *Zi Lang Hao* with hare hairs at the core and weasel's hair around, and *Bai Yun* with weasel's hair at the core and goat hairs around.

● 兼毫笔一套（清）
A set of *Jian Hao* brushes with mixed hairs (Qing Dynasty, 1644-1911)

兼毫笔种类

根据芯毫和披毫的比例不同，可制作出软硬程度不同的兼毫笔。以紫羊毫笔为例，有九紫一羊、七紫三羊、五紫五羊、三紫七羊、二紫八羊之分。

九紫一羊是用十分之九的紫毫为芯、十分之一的羊毫为披制成，笔头偏硬，适用于精工书写。

七紫三羊是用十分之七的紫毫为芯、十分之三的羊毫为披制成，笔头偏硬，适用于小楷的书写。

五紫五毫是用二分之一的紫毫为芯、二分之一的羊毫为披制成，软硬适中，适用于小楷的书写。

三紫七羊是用十分之三的紫毫为芯、十分之七的羊毫为披制成，笔头柔软，适用于中楷、小楷的书写。

二紫八毫是用五分之一的紫毫为芯、五分之四的羊毫为披制成，笔头柔软，适用于行书的书写。

Varieties of *Jian Hao* Brushes

Different ratios made different kinds of *Jian Hao*, or mixed-hair writing brushes. There were ninety percent of hare hairs plus ten percent of goat hairs, seventy percent of hare hairs plus thirty percent of goat hairs, half hare hairs and half goat hairs, thirty percent of hare hairs and seventy percent of goat hairs and twenty percent of hare hairs and eighty percent of goat hairs.

Ninety percent of hare hairs plus ten percent of goat hairs made a fairly hard tip good for writing smaller characters.

Seventy percent of hare hairs at the core plus thirty percent of goat hairs around made less hard tips, good for small characters in regular script writing.

Half hare hairs at the core plus half goat hairs around made medium hard tips, good for small characters in regular script writing.

Thirty percent of hare hairs at the core plus seventy percent goat hairs around made soft tips, ideal for medium and small characters in.

Twenty percent of hare hairs plus eighty percent of goat hairs made exceptionally soft tips, perfect for running script writing.

- **兼毫笔的制作方法——披柱法**
  披柱法是在芯毫外披上披毫，是较早的制笔方法，目前仍是中国毛笔制造的主要方法。
  Pi Zhu, making technique for *Jian Hao* brushes
  Pi Zhu was to cover the core hairs with another kind of hairs. This was a fairly early way to make writing brushes. Today, it is still frequently seen.

根据笔锋长短的不同，毛笔可以分为超长锋笔、长锋笔、中锋笔、短锋笔等几种。笔锋的长短直接影响着书写的效果。

超长锋笔弹性最大，富于变化，可根据书写者的要求随心所欲地写出浓淡变化不同的字体。长锋笔笔锋细长，吸墨性强，写出的字饱满圆润。短锋笔笔锋粗短，吸墨性弱，写出的字苍劲，风骨毕露。中锋笔介于长锋笔和短锋笔之间，适宜日常写作。

Writing brushes could also be categorized by the length of their tips, the super long, long, medium and short. Different lengths determined the looks of writing.

The super long was the most elastic and form-changeable, able to satisfy the need by writer's mood. After this was the long tip, which was very good for absorbing ink. The characters written with this kind of brushes were well-rounded in strokes. The short tip was picking up less ink but able to give an old and weathered look through thin but vigorous brushstrokes. The medium length tips were good for everyday use.

By different needs writing brushes

• 长锋笔
Long-tip writing brush

• 短锋笔
Short-tip writing brush

根据笔头的不同用途，毛笔又能分出抓笔、斗笔、柳叶笔、面相笔、提笔、屏笔、联笔等。

抓笔的形制短粗便于把持，需要抓在手里写。其毫毛一般用比较粗硬的猪鬃或马鬃制成，这种笔是写仿宋字的最大的笔。

had different kinds, holding brushes, *Dou Bi* brushes, salix-leaf brushes, face brushes, *Ti Bi* brushes, *Ping Bi* brushes, *Lian Bi* brushes... just to name a few.

The holding brush, as its name suggested, was held inside palm and its hairs were hard bristles or horse mane. This kind was the biggest for writing imitations of Song-style characters.

Dou Bi brushes were for bigger characters in regular script, often made with goat hairs or whisker.

Salix-leaf brushes got their name from their long and narrow shape like willow leaves. Their tip was long and thin, often used for small character writing or shades application to a drawing.

• 抓笔（明）
Holding writing brush (Ming Dynasty, 1368-1644)

斗笔用于书写比大楷再大些的字，多用长羊毫、羊须做成。

柳叶笔因形似柳叶而得名，笔杆纤细，笔锋狭长，多用于小字、铺染。

• 柳叶笔
Salix-leaf writing brush

面相笔是用来勾勒人物线条或者渗线用的一种极细的毛笔，多用于壁画、人物画的构图。

提笔是用猪毫做成的专供写匾额用的毛笔。

屏笔是写屏条用的笔，比提笔稍小一点，多用长毫做成，属于大楷笔类。

联笔就是专门用来写对联的毛笔，联笔毫毛的软硬常常根据字体所需来配比。

Face writing brushes were for very fine delineation of human figures, often seen in frescoes and portraits.

The *Ti Bi* brushes, made with bristles, were for inscription on boards.

Ping bi brushes were smaller than *Ti Bi*, often made with long tips for large characters in regular script.

Lian Bi brushes were for antithetical couplets on doorways and their hardness could change to follow the size of characters.

· 提笔（清）
Ti Bi writing brush (Qing Dynasty, 1644-1911)

> 笔中名品

在毛笔漫长的发展过程中，出现了许多著名的制笔工匠，他们对制笔工艺的改良和创新推动了制笔产业的发展。他们从事制笔事业的地区也因此名声大噪，这些地区制作的毛笔成为人们收藏的主要对象。

> Famous varieties:

Over the past history many famous makers appeared. They advanced the progress of making technology and the place they did business became famous. Writing brushes made in these places were collectables.

笔有四德

古人对选笔提出了四项基本标准，即笔的"四德"。笔有四德之说是由明代文人屠隆在《文具雅编》中首先提出来的，即好的毛笔应符合"尖、齐、圆、健"四项基本标准，即笔头尖、笔锋齐、笔身圆、毛体健。毛笔若有此四德，即便不是出自名家之手，也是上品佳作。

"尖"指笔毫的末端要尖利。将笔润湿后，毫毛聚拢时便可分辨尖秃。尖利的毛笔书写出来的点画自然、飘逸，气息灵动。

"齐"指将笔头用水润开，刮成扁平状后，笔毛须呈现出整齐均匀的状态。

• 笔有四德
The four virtues a nice writing brush should possess

"圆"指笔毫要圆实，无塌扁之处。这样才能保证书写时笔锋不会偏向一侧或随意绞转，影响书写效果。

"健"指毛笔笔腰应具有弹性。将笔重压后提起，随即恢复原状则说明毛笔有弹力，能够运用自如。

The Four Virtues a Nice Writing Brush Should Possess

Ancient people had four criteria when selecting a writing brush, which were described as "four virtues". This phrase was firstly put forward by Tu Long, a Ming-dynasty scholar, in his book *Wen Ju Ya Bian*, or "*Tools Used in the Study*". By him, a nice brush tip should be "pointed, neat, round and vigorous" at the same time. In other words, the tip end should be pointed, the hairs neat, the tip waist round and the tip's body strong and vigorously. Any brush with these four, even not from a master maker, was a nice one.

"Pointed" referred to the end of the tip. After moistened with ink, the hairs should stay neatly together with a pointed pinnacle. This pointed pinnacle enabled graceful, flowing and lively brushstrokes to happen.

"Neat" meant, when moistened with water, the tip became flat to show a very orderly shape.

"Round" meant round and solid hairs without irregularity in form. This round shape guaranteed the tip not to go astray when force was applied and no compromise in brushstrokes' looks.

"Vigorous" meant the waist of the tip should be elastic and able to bounce back to its original shape when the force applied was removed. This property guaranteed writing with ease.

李渡毛笔

江西进贤县李渡镇是中国著名的毛笔产地，至今已有1700多年的制笔历史。据说秦代蒙恬改良毛笔制作工艺以后，当时的咸阳人郭解和朱兴由中原来到江西李渡一带，传授制笔技艺，奠定了李渡制笔业的基础。李渡毛笔的特点是选材严格，品种繁多，式样新颖，大小齐

Writing Brushes Made in Lidu

Lidu, a town in Jinxian County of Jiangxi, is famous for making writing brushes for over 1700 years until now. After Meng Tian reformed the brush making technology, people say, Guo Jie and Zhu Xing, two natives from Xianyang, came from the central plain to settle down in Lidu, where they invented new technologies and taught students.

全，长短兼备，其毛笔精选各类毫毛，有狼毫、紫毫、鸡毫、羊毫、兼毫等，笔尖丰硕圆润；装潢有黑、白、花等笔管。笔锋有红、绿、黄、白、青、蓝、紫七色，其中"纯净紫毫"、"五羊紫毫"、"墨宝"、"墨翰"等为传统名笔。

Writing brushes made in this place featured tough material selection, more varieties to choose from, a complete production line in different specifications. Their source of hairs was extensive, hare, goat, rooster and weasel, either used alone or mixed. Their brush tips were rounding, full and hard, often to go with nice-looking color brush holders. Their brush tips, it was said, might be made in any color of a rainbow. Their dark hare, five-goat and jet-black varieties enjoyed a big reputation.

- "双羊牌"毛笔
  Writing brushes of "Double-goat" Brand

北京书画笔

北京书画笔因产于北京而得名，主要用于绘画领域。

到清朝中后期，北京的制笔业才逐渐兴旺起来，先后出现了吴文魁、韩殿安、胡魁章、陈富元等笔

Writing Brushes Made in Beijing for Painting and Calligraphy

Writing brushes made in Beijing are used mainly for painting.

Writing brush making made a progress in Beijing in the mid or late Qing Dynasty, with famous shops named

庄。清末民初又陆续出现了王文通、青莲阁、李福寿、崔林元、胡文升、王德和等笔庄。这些笔庄以生产销售低档笔为主，是北京书画笔的早期形态。

1925年，中国著名画家金北楼、齐白石、汤定之等人组成了"中国画学研究会"，在去日本访问后带回日本鸠居堂笔店所制的毛笔交李福寿研究试制。李福寿根据画家提出的要求，并针对各个画家的绘画特点，反复试验，改进了笔胎的衬垫方法和原材料，制成了独具特色的书画笔。此后，李福寿不断精研笔艺，从而使得李福寿画笔成为畅销全国的名品，由此奠定了北京书画笔在笔史上的地位。直到现在，北京书画笔的制作仍然沿用李福寿的工艺。

after their owners like Wu Wenkui, Han Dianan, Hu Kuizhang and Chen Fuyuan. More shops came by the end of the Qing Dynasty, or in the early years of the Republic. These shops as the early form of this trade in Beijing sold inexpensive brushes.

• 日本鸠居堂所制毛笔
Writing brushes made by Kyukyodo, Japan

• 北京书画笔
Painting and calligraphy brushes made in Beijing

- 《蟹图》齐白石（近代）
Crabs, by Qi Baishi (modern China)

In 1925, famous artists Jin Beilou, Qi Baishi and Tang Dingzhi formed an art association. They gave Li Fushou the brushes they had brought from Japan for a trial production. By their requirements, with their different artistic styles on mind, and after repeated experiments and improvements made on materials and cushions, Li Fushou did it, successfully made painting brushes with Beijing characteristics. Later, with repeated improvements his products became a hot item on domestic market. Thanks to his efforts, the painting and calligraphy brush made in Beijing won a place in China's brush making history. Even today, the brushes made in Beijing still follow his technology.

Writing brushes made by *Zou Zi Guang Ge*

Zou Zi Guang Ge in Wuhan is a hundred-year-old business in making writing brushes following a technique from Linchuan of Jiangxi (a famous making place in ancient China). In 1850, Zou Farong from Lijiadu of Linchuan came to Wuhan where he opened this shop. Later, a Qing-dynasty calligrapher, also an academician of the royal academy Li Duanqing, courtesy-named Taoist Qing,

邹紫光阁毛笔

武汉邹紫光阁是一家有百余年历史的名笔店，其制作技艺源于江西临川（古代制笔业发达之地）。1850年，临川李家渡人邹法荣到武汉开设笔店。清朝翰林、书法家李端清（又名清道人）为该店题写"紫光阁"横匾。在之后的百余年间，这家笔店几经兴衰，分为了成记、益记和久记三家，到新中国成立后尚存久记一家。武汉邹紫光阁毛笔以做工精细，选料考究，设计美观，古朴典雅，"尖、齐、圆、健"而闻名于世。

四川乐山宋笔

宋笔是一种写榜书匾额的大抓笔，产于四川省乐山市，因受宋代大文豪苏轼和黄庭坚赞誉而得名。

四川省乐山市古称嘉州。相传北宋时，嘉州凌云山新建了一座凉亭，当时正赶上大文豪苏轼在此游览。寺僧拿来当地特制的一支大抓

wrote for the shop its famous signboard. This business experienced ups and downs in the following hundred years, during which time it branched off into three: *Chengji*, *Yiji* and *Jiuji* but only *Jiuji* was still in business by the founding of New China. The writing brushes made by *Zou Zi Guang Ge* with the best material and in the best design have all the virtues a nice brush should have, having a simple but graceful look and able to meet all the four criteria: pointed, neat, round and vigorous.

Song Brushes from Leshan of Sichuan

The *Song* brush from Leshan of Sichuan is for big characters inscribed on horizontal boards. It got its name from the recommendation by literary giants Su Shi and Huang Tingjian of the Song Dynasty (960-1279).

In ancient times Leshan of Sichuan was called Jiazhou. During the Northern Song period (1127-1279), Su Shi came to the Lingyun Mount in Jiazhou, where a pavilion on top of the mount had just been completed. Some monk brought a locally made huge brush, asking Su Shi to write a name for the pavilion. Upon the request Su Shi wrote "the

笔，请苏轼为亭子赐名。苏轼题写了"清音亭"三个大字，并当众称赞该笔为良品。时隔不久，北宋书法家黄庭坚也到嘉州游览，也用大抓笔留下"中流砥柱"的墨宝。此后，大抓笔成为天下名笔，后世誉之为"宋笔"。

pavilion of pure music". He gave very high remarks to the brush's performance, describing it as "a very nice variety". Before long, Huang Tingjian came too, who used the same style product when doing a calligraphic work. After the two literary giants, this big holding brush became famous, known as *Song* brush to later generations.

● 《苦笋赋》【局部】黄庭坚（宋）
Ku sun fu (detail), by Huang Tingjian (Song Dynasty, 960-1279)

● 四川成都古玩市场里的各式毛笔
Varieties of writing brushes in an antique market of Chengdu, Sichuan Province

韩愈《毛颖传》

韩愈（768—824），唐代文学家。他的文章《毛颖传》，采用拟人的手法为毛笔立传。在文中，虚拟人物毛颖（即毛笔）被蒙恬俘获并献于秦始皇，被封管城子，得秦始皇宠爱，官至中书令。后来因为年老毫秃不中用，回到封邑，死于管城。文章以一支毛笔的产生、发展和废置为脉络，叙述了毛笔在历史文化上的作用，在歌颂毛笔卓越功勋的同时，讽刺了统治者的刻薄、寡情。

Story of Mao Ying by Han Yu

Han Yu (768-824), a Tang-dynasty essayist who wrote a biography *Story of Mao Ying* about writing brushes by a virtual character. Mao Ying (referring to the writing brush), after being captured by Meng Tian, was brought to Qin Shihuang, the First Emperor of Qin, who gave him a title. In royal favor he worked his way up to a high position until he lost hairs and became useless in old age. He returned to his manor and died there. While speaking highly of the function the writing brush performed in culture and literature, the story flogged a cruel and mean ruler.

笔墨纸砚
Writing Brush, Ink Stick, Paper and Ink Slab

- 韩愈像
  Han Yu

- 《毛颖传》韩愈（唐）
  Story of Mao Ying, by Han Yu (Tang Dynasty, 618-907)

黄昌典毛笔

"黄昌典"是广西桂林市的著名笔庄，从清朝中期开始营业，以创店人黄昌典的名字命名。黄昌典毛笔代表了桂林毛笔制作的最高水平，曾有"黄昌典，买笔不用选"的民谣流传。

据记载，黄昌典是清代咸丰年间的秀才，擅书画，科举考试落第后开始经营毛笔。由于桂林野兔较少，所以历来制笔多用鸡毛。黄昌典为了改变这种局面，从北方购得兔毛、狼毫，并专门从华东聘请制笔名师到桂林制笔，由此诞生了黄昌典笔庄，享誉岭南数百年。

- "黄昌典"牌羊毫对笔（现代）
  Huang Chang Dian goat-hair writing brushes (contemporary products)

Writing Brushes Made by Huang Changdian

Huang Chang Dian, named after its founder, was a famous business in writing brushes in Guilin of Guangxi Province since the mid Qing Dynasty (1644-1911). Their brushes were the best in Guilin. People said, "You needn't pick and choose, every one of theirs is the best you can get."

Huang Changdian, the founder, passed the royal examination on the county level during the Xianfeng Rein of the Qing Dynasty. After he failed in the examination on the provincial level he quit the pursuit for officialdom, but turned to commercial business by doing writing brushes. Because Guilin had fewer hares, brush makers had used chicken feathers instead. Huang Changdian changed this situation. He purchased hare and weasel hairs from the north and hired the best craftsmen he could get. His business enjoyed a tremendous fame for several hundred years.

汝阳刘毛笔

汝阳刘毛笔产于河南省汝阳刘村，相传此地秦汉时期即已产生制笔业，至今已有两千余年的历史。东晋大书法家王羲之曾用汝阳刘毛笔书写《黄庭经》，觉得此笔洒脱流畅，婉转自如，赞其为"妙笔"，从此该地有"妙笔之乡"的美誉。汝阳刘毛笔的特点是尖齐饱圆，锋颖尖锐、犹如锥状，经久耐用，且性能刚柔相济，挺拔有力，运笔流畅，深得历代书画家及文人墨客喜爱。

Writing Brushes from the Liu Village of Ruyang

The Liu Village of Ruyang, Henan Province, is said to begin making writing brushes during the Qin and the Han Dynasties over 2000 years ago. Famous calligraphy artist Wang Xizhi of the Eastern Jin Dynasty wrote the famous work *Taoist Sutra of Huang Ting* with a brush from this village. To him, that brush was perfect, which he described as "something not from this world",so this village gained a tremendous fame for many years to come. The brushes it made featured a very pointed shape able to last for a long time. Their tips were strong and soft, able to give a vigorous and flowing writing. Because of this they were in favor of scholars and artists alike.

• "满园春色"湖笔
"Garden Full of Spring Beauty" *Hu* style writing brush

掖县毛笔

山东掖县毛笔始于清代康熙年间，一直以用料讲究、做工精细、造型典雅著称。掖县毛笔选用福建凤眼竹和湖南湘妃竹等名竹作为笔管，并以粤、桂的黑水牛角作笔斗，其笔头选用东北黄鼠狼尾为主料，佐以适量香狸尾、兔须、鸡毛、豹毛和石獾尾等细尾毛制成。

- 竹子——笔管常用材料
  笔管的材料的质量也是影响毛笔品质的一个因素。
  Bamboo, the usual material for brush holders
  The material for the holder had much to do with the final quality of writing brushes.

Writing Brushes from the Yexian County

The Yexian County of Shandong Province enjoyed a big name in making writing brushes with the best materials available, painstaking technology and elegant appearance. Their holders were made with the best bamboo from Fujian and Hunan and the tip holder made with the horn from black buffalo from Guangdong and Guangxi. Their tips used weasel hairs from China's northeast only, reinforced by a small amount from leopard cat tail, hare, rooster feathers, leopard hairs and badger tails.

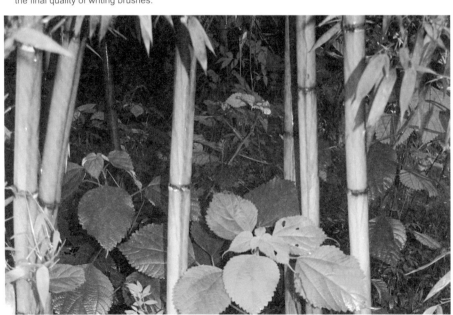

智永"退笔冢"

智永，隋朝僧人，晋代书法大家王羲之的第七世孙。

相传智永在游善琏镇时，住在镇上蒙恬祠边的永欣寺，一住就是三十年。在此期间，他潜心练习书法，临写了千余本《千字文》送于各寺庙。当时毛笔的笔头可以退下，也就是换笔头而保留原有的笔杆，称为"退笔"。智永几十年来退下的笔头积攒了十大筐，他让人在永欣寺窗前挖了一个大坑，埋这些笔头。由于所砌土堆像坟冢，得名"退笔冢"。智永大师圆寂后就埋葬在"退笔冢"旁边。智永"退笔冢"的故事成为后世勤学苦练的典范。

Monk Zhiyong and His Brush Tip Grave

Zhiyong, a monk of the Sui Dynasty (581-618), the seventh-generation grandson of the famous calligrapher Wang Xizhi.

He was said living in the Yongxin Temple for 30 years after he came to the town of Shanlian, a temple next to the memorial place for Meng Tian, during which time he practiced calligraphy by making a thousand copies of a classical book *Qian Zi Wen*, or *One Thousand Character Primer*, which he gave temples as gifts. The writing brushes he used had removable tips, which meant the writer could replace the used tip with a new one. The tips he had used over the thirty years were enough to fill ten baskets. He made a grave outside his window for these tips. He even gave the grave a name, "the tomb of used brush tips". After he died he had himself buried next to these tips. This story was often used to spur people for working harder.

● 退笔冢
The tomb of used brush tips

● 《千字文》【局部】智永（隋）
One Thousand Character Primer (detail), by Zhiyong (Sui Dynasty, 581-618)

侯店毛笔

在中国历史上，河北衡水素有"北国笔乡"之称，此地是中国著名的毛笔产地之一，以在明清时期生产宫廷用笔著称。侯店毛笔的特点是选料精良，做工精细，所制之笔锋长杆精，刚柔相济，含墨量多而不滴，行笔流畅而不滞。侯店毛笔笔管以角、骨、象牙、红木等材质为原料进行精雕细琢，管身饰以龙凤、花草、山水等图案，增强了整支毛笔的艺术性。

Writing Brushes from Houdian

In history, Hengshui of Hebei Province enjoyed a big name as "famous for making writing brushes", and its products were exclusively for the use of the royal families during the Ming and the Qing Dynasties. The best brushes from Hengshui were made in a village named Houdian, which featured long tips able to write fluent, vigorous and soft brushstrokes and elaborately wrought holders. They could pick more ink than other varieties and the ink on their tips never dripped. The materials used for brush holders were expensive stuff like animal horns and bones, ivory or rosewood. They were often inscribed with dragon, phoenix, flower or bird or landscape to highlight an artistic taste.

• 鲨鱼骨、兽骨杆羊毫笔（清）
Brushes made with goat hairs and holders of shark or other animal's bone (Qing Dynasty, 1644-1911)

周虎臣毛笔

上海周虎臣笔厂是一家拥有三百余年历史的老笔庄，于清朝康熙年间在苏州以"周虎臣笔墨庄"的店名创店。周虎臣笔庄以生产狼毫书画笔、狼毫水笔著称，不仅具备"尖、齐、圆、健"的特点，而且锋颖锐利，圆润饱满，刚劲有力，经久耐用，富有弹性。部分毛笔还以湘妃竹、红木、景泰蓝、象牙等多种名贵材质为笔管，精心装饰，观赏性极强。

Writing Brushes Zhou Huchen Made

This factory in Shanghai is three hundred years old, founded during the Kang Xi Rein of the Qing Dynasty. The best known variety it made was weasel hair brushes for painting and writing, with tips of all the four virtues, pointed, neat, round and vigorous. The sides of their tips were sharp like a knife and this was for writing vigorous brushstrokes. Also, they were elastic and endurable. Some of the holders were made with expensive materials like rare bamboo varieties, rosewood, ivory or cloisonné enamel, very pretty to look at.

• 景泰蓝羊毫笔（清）
Goat hair brushes with cloisonné enamel (Qing Dynasty, 1644-1911)

毛笔的保养

　　一支值得收藏的毛笔，要很好的保养才能保持它的价值。如果保养不得当，可能导致毛笔损坏，影响毛笔的经济价值和艺术价值。

　　如果是使用过的毛笔，一定要将笔毫上的墨汁或颜料洗净，并及时晾干。若有笔帽，可在晾干后套上。如果是未使用过的毛笔，则无需清洗。

　　毛笔的存放有挂放、卧放、盒放三种方式。值得收藏的毛笔一般采用盒放，一般为一支毛笔或一套毛笔置于一个盒中。挂放和卧放适用于档次较低的毛笔。

- 洗净的毛笔要用笔帽套好
  Brushes, after being washed clean, must be capped.

- 毛笔存放方法之盒放
  Be boxed

How to Take Care of Writing Brushes

A nice writing brush needs good care. Otherwise, they would be damaged and lose their economic and artistic values.

After use, they have to be washed clean without ink or paint left on the tip, then dried by airing and being capped. An unused writing brush doesn't have to do this.

They can be kept in three ways when not in use: be hung up, laid down or boxed. Expensive brushes are often boxed, usually, one box for one or one set. Hanging and laying flat are for less expensive brushes.

● 毛笔存放方法之挂放
Be hung up

墨

Ink Stick

　　墨是一种黑色块状的研磨颜料，广泛应用于书写、绘画、拓碑等方面。墨的使用，大大改善了文字的储存条件，加快了文字传播和演化的速度，也使中国古代书画拥有了独特的艺术风格。墨作为文房四宝之一，为中华文化的传播做出了巨大的贡献。

Ink sticks are ink in a solid form to be ground for writing, painting and rubbing. The use of it tremendously helped the store, spreading and evolution of written characters, giving traditional Chinese painting and calligraphy a very unique and highly artistic look. As one of the four treasures of the study, the contribution ink sticks have made to the development of Chinese culture cannot be overestimated.

> 墨的历史

墨在中国的历史源远流长，从最初的天然石墨到人工墨，再到各种材质、各种形状、各种功能的精美墨品，以及现在所用的墨汁，中国墨经历了漫长的发展历程。

墨的起源

墨的使用可以追溯到原始社会，那时人们就开始用天然的有色

• 石墨
石墨是一种原始的天然墨。
Graphite
Graphite is a primitive form of natural ink.

> History of Ink Stick

Ink sticks have a long history in China, beginning from their initial form of natural graphite to man-made nice looking ones of different materials, different shapes and for different purposes.

Origin of Ink Stick

Back to the primitive society people used colored minerals for painting and these minerals made the embryo form of ink sticks. In 1980, the black-red mineral unearthed from a Yangshao Cultural site of Lintong, Shaanxi Province, proved beyond any doubt the use of primitive ink used in painting. The ink seen on turtle shells and animal bones with inscribed letters from the Shang Dynasty (1600 B.C.-1046 B.C.) was commonly taken as the earliest mark ink left in history. Though

矿石作画，这些有色矿石可以看作是墨的雏形。1980年，陕西临潼姜寨村仰韶文化遗址中出土的黑红色矿石，证明了原始墨在彩绘上的应用。商代甲骨上留有的天然石墨的痕迹，被认为是最早的墨迹。天然矿石虽然与后来的墨有很大区别，但已经具备墨的书画功能，原始人用它们绘出红、黄、黑、白等不同的颜色。天然墨包括天然产出的黑色颜料，如树木燃烧后遗留下的有机物炭质、烟炱，动植物分泌物，以及黑土和有色矿石等。

西周时期，人工墨开始出现。据古书《述古书法纂》记载："邢夷始制墨，字从黑土、煤烟所成，土之类也。"邢夷是西周宣王时期人，这标志着西周时期开始人工制墨。由于人工墨在质量和数量上远胜天然墨，这使得墨的大量运用成为可能。人工墨的出现是墨史的第一个转折点。

- 隶书"墨"字
  墨，从土从黑。
  The character "ink" written in the clerical script
  Ink, following soil, is black in color.

minerals differed a lot from the ink that appeared later, they were able to satisfy the need for painting, and with them primitive people did red, yellow, black and white. Natural ink included black stuff existent in nature like the organic charcoal from burnt wood, soot, secretions from animals, black soil and colored minerals.

Man made ink appeared during the Western Zhou Dynasty (1046 B.C.-771 B.C.) and the history book *Ancient Calligraphy* says, "Xing Yi was the first maker of man-made ink and he did it from black soil and soot." Xing Yi lived during the King Xuan's reign, which marked the beginning of man-made ink of his time. Because man-made ink was better in quality and larger in quantity, its popularity was a sure thing. So, the man-made ink had its first milestone in history.

春秋战国时期，墨的使用已经较为普遍。同期出土的实物竹简、木牍、帛书上的文字，经考证有许多是用毛笔蘸墨书写的。战国文献中还记载了关于墨的使用情况，如《尚书·吕刑》中有关于"墨罚"的记载，这是一种以刀划破面部，再在伤口处涂墨的刑罚，这种刑罚留下的印痕终身难以脱落。

By the Spring and Autumn Period (770 B.C.-221 B.C.) the use of ink was common. Many unearthed inscribed bamboo or wood strips or writings on silk had characters written with ink by writing brushes. Some books from the Warring States Period documented its use. A history book *Shang Shu: Lv Xing*, or *Collection of Ancient Texts*, recorded a torture criminals received then: his face was cut by knife and ink was rubbed into the cuts so the stain stayed forever.

● 木牍（秦）
木牍上的文字是用毛笔蘸墨书写的。
Wood strips with written characters (Qin Dynasty, 221 B.C.-206 B.C.)
The writing was done by a writing brush with ink.

与墨有关的词语

墨在中国古代与学问有关，因使用墨来进行书画的都是文人，所以与墨有关的词语多与文人或才华有关。如：

【墨客】指风雅的文人。

【舞文弄墨】指玩弄文字，含贬义。

【胸无点墨】比喻没有文化。

【笔墨功夫】指做文章的本领。

Phrases Related to Ink

Ink was closely related to book learning in ancient times and everyone who used ink to write was described as men of letters. So ink was related to artistic or literary talents.

"*mo ke*", refers to scholars with a graceful manner

"*wu wen nong mo*" refers to being unnecessarily playful with words, a derogative term.

"*xiong wu dian mo*" means having no learning.

"*bi mo gong fu*" means the ability for article writing.

● **泼墨仙人图 梁楷（宋）**

墨是中国古代画家用来作画的最主要的材料。

Immortal, ink-splash style painting, by Liang Kai (Song Dynasty, 960-1279)

Ink was the most important tool to artists of ancient times.

秦汉时期的墨

秦汉时期，制墨业最发达的地方是隃糜（今陕西千阳）、延州（今陕西延安）、扶风（今陕西凤翔）等地，其中以隃糜产墨最为著名，后世还以隃墨作为墨的别称。秦代的墨多为墨丸，为团状或短小的圆柱状，使用时要放在砚台上用研石压磨。因此早期的砚台都附有研石，直到东汉时才出现能直接在砚上研磨的两头细、中间粗的"握子"形墨。

● 古砚和古墨（秦）
出土于湖北云梦睡虎地秦墓中的古墨残块，是目前可见最早的墨。
Ancient ink slab and ink stick (Qin Dynasty, 221 B.C.-206 B.C.)
This broken piece off an ancient ink stick unearthed from a Qin tomb is taken as the oldest ink stick ever discovered.

Ink Made During the Qin and the Han Dynasties

During the Qin and the Han Dynasties (221 B.C.-220 A.D.) ink making was mostly seen in present-day Qianyang, Yan'an and Fengxiang of Shaanxi Province, respectively called Yumi, Yanzhou and Fufeng in ancient times. Of all, the ink made in Yumi enjoyed the biggest fame. The name of Yumi was even used to stand for the best ink. Ink made during the Qin was small balls or cylinders, and when used, was ground against a stone. So ink slabs in early stage often went with a stone stick for convenient grounding, a stick used to pin the ink from rolling away. This practice lasted until the Eastern Han Dynasty, when the shape of the ink took a change: smaller on both ends but bigger on the waist for easy holding.

During the Han Dynasty ink making was a valued trade by the government. It had positions to take charge of anything related to paper, ink stick and writing

汉代时制墨业已受到统治者的重视，政府不仅专门设置了专门掌管纸、墨、笔等物的官职，而且还向文官按月发放墨块。据文献记载，汉代文职官员每月可领得"隃糜大墨一枚，小墨一枚"。

brush. Each month, the government issued ink sticks to its civil officials. How many could they get? By history books, each got a big piece and a small piece per month.

"临池学书，池水尽墨"

"临池学书，池水尽墨"是一个典故，说的是东汉书法家张芝的故事。

张芝，擅长草书，有"草圣"之称。相传张芝练字以帛为纸，临池学书，将写过的帛在池塘里洗净后再用，久而久之，池塘水都变成了黑色。后人便将"池水尽墨"当做勤奋好学的象征。

After Years of Calligraphy Practice by a Pond, the Pond Water Became Jet Black

This is a story about Zhang Zhi, an Eastern Han Dynasty man.

The running script was his strong hand and he enjoyed a name "Sage of Cursive Script". When he was young he practiced calligraphy on silk by a pond, and every day he washed the silk covered with writing in the pond for a fresh use the next day. After a long time the pond water became jet black. Later generations took this as encouragement for hard learning.

墨模

墨模是制墨时用来压制墨块成型的专用模具，多以石楠木、棠梨木制成，也有的以金属制成。墨模诞生于东汉时期，其出现为规模化制墨带来了可能，制墨业因此得到长足发展。墨模见证着墨的发展变化，许多珍贵的墨都是通过墨模制造而成。有的墨模本身也是艺术精品，比较著名的有"御制西湖名胜图墨墨模"、"御制棉花图墨墨模"、"新安大好山水墨墨模"、"御制四库文阁诗墨墨模"等。

● 古代墨模
Ink moulds from ancient times

东汉发明墨模后，应用并不多。从唐代到元代这段时期，墨模较简单，基本形式是多模一锭，即制作一锭墨需要多个墨模的配合。明代时，墨模得到改进，制模方式从多模一锭变成一模一锭，即将几块墨印合成于一个六面嵌套的总模具之中，每面上均有手工镂刻的纹样和文字。清代的墨模更加精美，雕刻技法非常高超，很多墨工穷其一生只能制作2～3副墨模。总的来说，明清的墨模艺术性很高，是制墨业发展巅峰时期的衍生物。

● 西湖十景墨（清）
Ten scenes of the West Lake (Qing Dynasty, 1644-1911)

Mould for Ink Sticks

The ink mould was for ink clay to take shape in sizable production. Most moulds were made with expensive and very strong woods, some, with metal. The earliest mould appeared in the Eastern Han Dynasty (25-220). With the moulds ink stick production gained a fast progress. The mould was a witness to the progress, even a parent of ink because without the moulds, many precious ink forms would simply fail to be born. Some moulds, in themselves, were works of art. Among the best ones from ancient times are "the scenes of West Lake" "the mould for cotton growing for royal use only" "landscape of Xin'an" and "the mould of royal library for classical writings".

The use of ink mould was less popular after its birth during the Eastern Han Dynasty. Even between the Tang Dynasty (618-907) and the Yuan Dynasty (1279-1368) they were simple and making a single stick took more than one mould to finish. Things changed during the Ming Dynasty, when one mould was enough for an ink stick to complete, which is to say making several sticks by a six-sided mould at one go, each of the sides having an inscription elaborately done by hand. Moulds made during the Qing Dynasty (1644-1911) became even more elaborate and impressive by a surprising technique. Some makers might spend entire life on just a couple. It was a widely accepted belief that moulds were more artistically shaped during the Ming and the Qing Dynasty. They were a side product when ink stick progress reached a zenith.

• 棉花图墨（清）
Moulds patterned with cotton (Qing Dynasty, 1644-1911)

魏晋南北朝时期的墨

魏晋南北朝时期是墨发展的重要时期。这一时期，以松枝或松树树干烧烟制成的松烟墨完全取代了天然的石墨。制墨业最发达的地方是易州（今河北易县）。易州地区出产优质松树，因此盛产质地上乘的松烟墨。

三国时期，魏国书法家韦诞在前人制墨的基础上进行了创新，制墨时在原料中加入鸡蛋、珍珠粉和麝香等材料，从而使得制成的墨香味独特、光泽持久，具有"一点如漆"的效果。魏晋南北朝时期，墨的制作工艺已经成熟，贾思勰在《齐民要术》中第一次系统地记载了制墨工艺。

Ink Sticks Made During the Wei, Jin, Southern and Northern Periods

Wei, Jin, Southern and Northern Periods (220-589) were crucial in the history of ink stick making. By then, pine soot ink from burnt pine leaves and trunks had replaced minerals as the material. Yizhou (present-day Yixian County of Hebei Province) had more ink making activities than any other place of China. The soot ink it produced was the best quality out of nice pine trees there.

Wei Dan, a calligrapher of the State of Wei during the Three Kingdoms Period (220-280) made a significant innovation on ink making by adding egg, pearl powder and musk to the material. Ink thus made had a very nice smell, shining and jet black in color. The making technique was matured during Wei, Jin, the Southern and Northern Periods. For the first time ever in history, ink making was documented by Jia Sixie in his famous book *Qi Min Yao Shu*, or *The Encyclopedia of Agriculture*.

● 制墨图
Ink Making

墨的制作过程

古代制墨全部采用手工制作，要经过炼烟、用胶、和料、制模、压模、晾干、加工等工艺流程，才能制出符合书写和收藏要求的好墨。

炼烟：是取烟炱的过程。它是用不完全燃烧的方法从松枝或油脂中提取烟尘，得到松烟或油烟。

用胶：用胶的好坏直接影响着墨的质量，胶分为鱼鳔胶、牛皮胶等多种，用法各有不同。古人熔胶要求胶水清澈可鉴，这样制成的墨才不腻。

和料：先将烟料和胶融合熬制，再投入色素原料和配料，同时用杵锤炼，做成料坯。

制模：就是做模具，墨工先设计好图纸，再将木料雕刻成墨模。墨模的形制大小和纹理十分重要，各流派的做法都密不外传。

压模：将初制墨锭压紧成形的一道工序。初制墨锭必须用一种叫"担"的工具压它，能使其周围结实，棱角规整，纹饰清晰，基本成型。

晾干：墨成型后要平放晾干。在初期，墨要不断翻转，使自然拱翘的墨体自行恢复平整，然后将墨放入石灰，出灰的时间要求恰到好处，墨才能不软不硬。再经过扎吊，这对于温度、湿度的控制很严格，过分干燥或湿度过大都会影响墨的质量。

加工：晾干后的墨锭只是初具形态，表面有很多毛刺和疙瘩，还需要对其进行加工才能使墨的表面平整圆润。然后是加漆衣，这是一道刮磨工艺，而不是真的在墨的表面涂漆，其目的是使墨更具光彩。最后是描金填彩。描金一般以金色和银色为主，能使墨品光亮。描金的作用不仅是好看，而且有密封作用，使墨保持一定的湿润度。加工的最后一步是制盒和包装。根据墨的形状配制纸盒、锦盒、漆盒等进行包装，墨的制作就此完成。

The Process of Ink Making

Everything was done by hand in ancient times. Every step in the process, from soot making, glue application, materials mixing, mould making, shaping to drying and finishing, concerned the final quality in writing and the value as collectables.

Soot making: this was to get soot from incomplete burning on pine leaves or grease.

Glue application: the quality of glue applied determined the quality of final product. The glue used was in different varieties like the fish glue and ox hide clue. Different type had different ways to apply. When melted, ancient people believed, the glue had to be a clear liquid and only liquid like this guaranteed ink not sticky.

Materials mixture: this was to mix soot and glue with color pigments added. The mixture was pounded repeatedly until it became a fine paste.

Mould making: by a pre-made design the mould was made out of wood and with carvings. The shape and veins on the mould were crucial and each school had secrets never made public.

Pressing: this step was to make the ink paste into the shape desired. The pressing was done by a tool called "*dan*" to make sure all the edges were solid, corners clean and patterns sharp.

Drying: this was to dry up the sticks. Repeated turning over was required at first and this was to get rid of warps. After this, the ink stick was left in lime for a length of time. The time to be taken out was crucial for correct hardness. After this was the step of hanging, which required right temperature and humid.

Finishing: dried-up sticks needed polishing to make surface smooth before they received a lacquer coat. Receiving a lacquer coat didn't mean as the name suggested, it was smoothening for a shining look. The last step was to receive a gold or silver color and this was to make the stick look nice. But there was something more to it: by sealing the ink from air it was able to keep right moisture. Finally, it was packaging with paper, brocade or lacquer containers.

隋唐时期的墨

隋唐时期，制墨技术已经十分成熟，这一时期制墨业空前兴盛，制墨技艺高超，名匠辈出，制墨中心从陕西地区扩大到山西、河北。易州（今河北易县）与潞州（今山西长治）是隋唐时期制墨业最发达的两个地方，它们最终成为隋唐时期的制墨中心。

Ink Sticks Made During the Sui and the Tang Dynasties

By the Sui and the Tang Dynasties (581-907) ink making technology was matured with master makers appearing. The places that made ink sticks were no longer limited to Shaanxi but expanded to Shanxi and Hebei. Yizhou, present-day the Yixian County of Hebei Province and Luzhou of today's Changzhi of Shanxi Province were famous two, eventually to replace Shaanxi as the center of this trade.

● 朱砂柱形墨（清）
朱砂墨多用于修改文稿或点校图书。
Cinnabar cylinder of ink stick (Qing Dynasty, 1644-1911)
Cinnabar ink was for book editing and annotating.

• 《兰亭序》（摹本）【局部】褚遂良（唐）

Lan Ting Xu, a copy (detail) made by Chu Suiliang (Tang Dynasty, 618-907)

在成型工艺方面，墨模完全取代了手工捣杵，因此制成的墨更加坚实耐用，形状也更加多样。在装饰方面，工匠可用墨印将文字、图案印于墨锭上，这样制出的墨更具艺术表现力。

唐代时还出现了有色墨，以黄墨和朱墨最为有名。黄墨是用雌黄研细加胶合制而成，朱墨是将朱砂研细后加胶制成。有色墨多用于修改文稿或者点校图书。

Shaping by hand was replaced by moulds and the sticks thus made were solid, endurable and in more shapes. Decorative characters and patterns could be printed for a better look.

By the Tang Dynasty color ink varieties appeared, among them, the most famous being the yellow and red. The yellow ink was made from orpiment powder with glue, while the red ink from cinnabar in very fine power with glue. These color inks were for book editing and annotating.

由于唐朝后期北方战乱频繁，大批手工艺人南迁。在制墨名家奚超的带领下，奚氏家族举家从易州迁往歙州（今安徽省黄山一带）。歙州盛产的松树品质不凡，适宜制墨。奚超在此制作出丰肌腻理、光泽如漆的松烟墨，歙州也取代原料殆尽的易州成为新的制墨中心。

五代时奚超之子奚廷珪出任南唐的墨务官，对制墨工艺进行改进，在墨料中加入多味中草药，在胶料中又添加了漆，这样制成的墨质坚纹细、防腐防蛀，书写时流畅不滞，并带有沁人的香气。酷爱书画的南唐后主李煜喜爱其墨，赐奚廷珪以国姓"李"，即李廷珪，自

Due to frequent wars in the northern part of China, many ink makers escaped to the south, bringing their skills along. Xi Chao was one of them who brought his family from Yizhou of Hebei to Shezhou of Anhui. With the good-quality pine trees in Shezhou, Xi Chao was able to make the best ink he had ever made and Shezhou replaced Yizhou as the major making place of the country. The pine resource was almost drained in the latter.

After Xi Chao's son Xi Tinggui became the official in charge of ink making, he innovated on the technology by adding Chinese medicinal herbs and lacquer into the glue. The ink made became finer in texture, more mothproof and resistant to decay, and very flowing in writing. On top of these virtues was

● **李煜像**

李煜（937—978），五代十国时期的南唐国君，世称李后主、南唐后主。他不通政治，国破降宋，但在文化艺术方面，他不仅精通书画，在诗词方面也有颇深的造诣，留下了《虞美人》、《浪淘沙》等千古杰作。

Li Yu

Li Yu (937-978) was the ruler of the Southern Tang Dynasty. As a statesman he was unqualified—he lost his kingdom to the Song ruler; but as an artistic and literary man he was a genius, leaving behind quite a number of immortal works in painting, calligraphy and poetry.

此"李墨"名扬天下。"李墨"的出现，是中国制墨工艺趋向成熟的标志。

宋元时期的墨

宋代制墨工艺进入普及阶段，河北、河南、山西、山东、安徽、四川等地均制墨，涌现出诸多制墨名家，其中以歙州制墨最为兴盛。宋宣和年间，宋徽宗下旨将"歙州"改为"徽州"，"徽墨"由此得名。

● 徽州风光
徽州交通便捷，物产丰富，是产墨的名地。
Landscape in Huizhou
Huizhou with easy transportation and many natural resources had every reason to be a famous ink making place.

a very nice fragrance it gave. Li Yu, ruler of the Southern Tang Dynasty, a tremendous painting and calligraphy lover, had a special likeness for this ink variety. He even went so far as to bestow Xi Tinggui, inventor of this variety, the royal family name of Li. The ink he made was named "the Li's ink". The fine quality of this ink variety marked the maturity of ink making in China.

Ink Sticks Made During the Song and the Yuan Dynasties

Ink making became popular during the Song Dynasty (960-1279), with many places doing it in Hebei, Henan, Shanxi, Shandong, Anhui and Sichuan. Many master makers appeared. Among all, ink making in Shezhou was more active. Emperor Huizong of the Song Dynasty, during his reign of Xuanhe, changed the name of Shezou to Huizhou. The famous *Hui* ink got its name.

The biggest contribution from the *Song* ink was the invention of soot ink made with tung oil, which exceeded previous variety in blackness, light reflection, permeability and stableness. The Song Dynasty also had a lacquer soot variety made from coal, grease

宋代出现了以桐油炼制的油烟墨，其在黑度、光泽、渗透性、稳定性等方面都远胜于松烟墨。宋代还出现了以松煤加杂脂、漆末烧烟制成的漆烟墨，精黑发亮，用来作画经久不褪。

• 宋墨
Song-dynasty ink sticks

宋墨不仅讲究选料精、墨色佳，而且讲究墨香和形制。宋代名墨工张遇在油烟墨中添加龙脑、麝香、金箔等制成贡御墨。歙州墨工潘谷改进配方和造型，制成的墨被誉为"墨中的神品"，苏轼尊称他为"墨仙"。

• 苏轼像
苏轼（1037—1101），号东坡居士，世称苏东坡，北宋文学家、书画家。
Su Shi
Su Shi (1037-1101), alias Dongpo, a famous literary man, painter and calligrapher of the Northern Song Dynasty.

and lacquer powder from burning. This variety was jet black and shining. Painting done with this ink lasted much longer before fading.

Song-dynasty ink featured tough material selection and final good appearance. It also laid much stock in fragrance. With precious items like borneol, musk and golden foil Pan Gu of Shezhou made the legendary type by an improved formula. This type was described as something from heaven and its maker Pan Gu the "ink god" by literary giant Su Shi.

宋代文人不仅喜墨，也尝试制墨，关心制墨工艺，留下了不少有关墨的著作，如苏易简的《文房四谱》、晁补之的《墨经》等，对后世制墨工艺、鉴定与收藏墨都起到了促进作用。

元朝时，制墨工匠受到蒙古统治者的民族压迫，身份卑微，制墨业的发展受到抑制，和宋代相比并没有太多的技术创新。徽州仍是传统的制墨中心。随着油烟墨产量的快速增长，松烟墨开始渐渐被油烟墨取代。就工艺来说，元代墨模的雕刻风格更加浑朴雄健，制墨工匠除了追求精湛的墨艺之外，也更注重墨的艺术性。

Song-dynasty scholars loved ink sticks, even tried to make their own. They put much effort and concern in its technology. Some of their writings were devoted to ink making, Su Yijian's *The Four Treasures of the Study* and Chao Buzhi's *Ink Classical* being two of them. These books helped later generations' appraisal and collection of ink sticks.

During the Yuan Dynasty (1279-1368), the cruel oppression from the Yuan government put ink makers at the bottom of society. The progress at making technology stood still, making almost no breakthrough from the Song technology. Huizhou was still the center of this trade. With the fast growth of ink made from tung soot, ink made from pine leaves lost market. However, ink moulds made a change: the Yuan moulds exhibited a bolder and more vigorous style. Apart from continuous efforts for perfection, ink makers turned their eyes to artistic values.

• 《北游帖》苏东坡（宋）
Trip Made in the North, calligraphic work by Su Dongpo (Song Dynasty, 960-1279)

文人自制墨

文人自制墨始于魏晋时期的韦诞，他结合前人的经验，创制了"一点如漆"的人工松烟墨，开创了制墨新思路。

唐代著名篆书家李阳冰的自制墨被誉为"坚泽如玉"；宋代文豪苏轼自制墨采用高丽煤、契丹胶，而且自认为其所制之墨可与李廷珪、张遇之墨相媲美；此外，当时的陆游、黄庭坚也有制墨尝试。

明清时期，自制墨达到高峰期，如纪晓岚的"双弈道人吟诗之墨"、阮元的"研经室校书墨"、刘墉的"清爱堂墨"、金农的"五百斤油"墨、梁启超的"饮冰室用墨"等，各具特色，精彩纷呈，反映出当时文人的心志和意趣。

Ink Sticks Made by Book Readers

This practice began from Wei Dan during the Wei and the Jin Periods (220-420). From the formula of previous generations he developed a new kind from pine leaves but blacker and glossier. His innovation gave much for professional makers to think about.

The ink sticks calligraphy Li Yangbing of the Tang Dynasty made were described as "solid and shining like jade". Song literary giant Su Shi made his from coal from Korea and glue from Khitan. To him, his ink was as good as the ink by Li Tinggui and Zhang Yu. His contemporaries Lu You and Huang Tingjian also made theirs.

This do-it-by-yourself game reached a peak during the Ming and the Qing Dynasties(1368-1911). Famous scholars like Ji Xiaolan, Ruan Yuan, Liu Yong, Jin Nong and Liang Qichao, all made theirs to be proud of and to show their fine taste.

- 金农像
  Jin Nong

- "五百斤油"墨
  Ink stick with "250 kilos of oil"

明清时期的墨

明代出现了规模较大的制墨作坊，制墨产业规模化、正规化，墨品的产量和质量得到提高，也促进了制墨品牌的形成。当时开墨坊、墨店的人增多，在流派上出现了"歙派"和"休宁派"。"歙派"以歙县的罗小华、程君房、方于鲁等为代表，制墨风格富丽堂皇、追求高古。"休宁派"以休宁的汪中山、邵格之为主将，制墨风格质朴，注重实用。

Ink Sticks from the Ming and the Qing Dynasties

Workshops appeared during the Ming Dynasty (1368-1644) and their production became sizable, almost like from an industry. Both varieties and qualities reached a level never obtained before. Brands appeared and more people entered this business. In style, ink sticks had different schools like the She and *Xiuning*. The she school represented by Luo Xiaohua, Cheng Junfang and Fang Yulu featured a luxurious and ancient look, while the *Xiuning* school with Wang Zhongshan and Shao Gezhi as representatives impressed by a look of

• 朱子家训墨（明）
Ink sticks inscribed with Zhu Family Teachings (Ming Dynasty, 1368-1644)

• 五鸟叙伦墨（明）
Ink Sticks with a bird pattern (Ming Dynasty, 1368-1644)

明墨的质量和品种较前代都有很大的提升，墨品更为坚细，锋可裁纸。明墨在造型、纹饰和包装等方面都更加追求美观，不再是单纯的实用品，很多都成为令人惊叹的艺术珍品。

elegant simplicity, more for practical use.

Ming ink had a much better quality than before, more refined, and more clear-cut in shape, "its edge" was said able to cut paper like a knife. In both shaping, decoration and wrapping, Ming ink made a big step forward. They were no longer only for practical use but

明代徽墨四大家

The Four Best-known *Hui* Style Makers During the Ming Dynasty

罗小华

明墨歙派的代表人物，擅长制造油烟墨，他制墨用桐油并加入"金珠玉屑"等材料，使墨坚如石，黑如漆。罗小华曾得到嘉靖皇帝的赞赏，官至中书舍人。罗小华的墨品传世稀少，其主要代表墨品有"小道士墨"等二十几种。

Luo Xiaohua

Representative of the *She* school, a master hand in tung oil ink making. With gold and jade added to materials the ink he made was as hard as stone and as black as lacquer. With the royal favor from Emperor Jiajing he served as an official in the court. Few of his works have come down in history, the best known including "Little Taoists".

程君房

明代歙派制墨名家。他是歙墨的集大成者，被誉为"李廷珪后第一人"。他创造了漆烟制墨法。其所制之墨研后滴于桌面，反复擦拭都不见褪色，被赞"入木三分，超过墨漆"。程君房制墨质地优良，墨的品相出众，墨模的绘画和雕刻均出自名家之手，款式和图案都新颖精美，深得文人士大夫的喜爱，最有名的是"玄元灵气"墨。

Cheng Junfang

Another master maker in *She* style, the inventor of the lacquer soot, taken as "the best maker after Li Tinggui". A drop of his ink on desk, people said, wouldn't come off even you wiped hard with a towel. Beside fine quality, the ink sticks he made possessed a very impressive look from a mould cut or inscribed by a famous artist. His works were very much sought after by scholars. Among his famous products was "The Fundamental Elements of the Heaven and Earth".

- 程君房制烂柯图墨（明）
Go-chess Game picture ink stick,
by Cheng Junfang (Ming Dynasty,
1368-1644)

方于鲁

明代著名墨工，明墨歙派的代表人物之一。方于鲁曾是程君房家中的匠人，学到了程氏制墨法后自立门户。方于鲁制墨技艺高超，创造性地改革了不少制墨流程，其最有名的墨品是"九玄三极墨"，此墨代表了方于鲁制墨的最高水准，受到众多文人的推崇。方氏与程氏两位制墨大家的竞争，促进了明代制墨业的发展。

Fang Yulu

Another She style representative was Fang Yulu, who had served as a servant in Cheng Junfang's family. After he learnt the skill he left to start his own business. He did many innovations on the making technology. The best known of his product was "the Nine Directions and Three Ends Ink", the best he ever made, a man-made marvel to numerous people. The competition between him and Cheng boosted the ink making technology of the Ming Dynasty.

邵格之

明墨休宁派的创始人之一。他擅长制作集锦墨，得名师真传，制造的墨品貌繁多，质地如玉，极具艺术性和观赏性。其所制墨品都留有自己的款识，代表作有"元黄天符"、"墨精"、"清都玉"、"功臣券"、"葵花墨"、"古风柱"、"梅花妙品"、"紫金霜"、"神品"等，现在传世的有"文玩"、"世宝"、"蟠螭"等。

Shao Gezhi

Founder of the *Xiuning* School, a master maker in making sets rather than individual sticks. He had many varieties to his name and all were highly artistic. Everything he made bore his name. Among the sticks he made only a few came down in history.

清代制墨业更加繁盛，以"徽墨"为代表的制墨业有了更进一步的发展，墨坊林立，墨在数量、质量、工艺技术、装饰、品相等方面均远远超越明代，达到了前所未有的高度。清代徽墨以曹素功、汪近圣、汪节庵、胡开文四大家为代表。

清代除了生产实用墨外，还生产观赏墨、彩墨、药墨等品种。

became collectables with artistic values.

The Qing Dynasty (1644-1911) saw a booming in business. The *Hui* style progressed further, surpassing the previous Ming in quantity, quality, technology, decoration and looks. The best known four in Huizhou then were Cao Sugong, Wang Jinsheng, Wang Jiean and Hu Kaiwen.

Apart from ink for practical use, the Qing Dynasty had color ink sticks, sticks for appreciation only and medicinal sticks.

During the prosperous Kang Xi and Qian Long reigns, ink makers invented new types for both practical use and artistic appreciation. Ink making for royal use gained a faster progress during the Qian Long reign.

At the end of the Qing Dynasty, Xie Songdai and Xie Songliang opened the famous *Yi De Ge* ink store in Beijing to

• 乾隆御咏名花诗十色墨（清）
The ten-color ink sticks of Emperor Qian Long, bearing the poem he composed for flowers (Qing Dynasty, 1644-1911)

"康乾盛世"期间，制墨工匠精雕细琢，不断推陈出新，集实用与艺术价值于一体的御墨得到发展。乾隆年间，御墨的制作工艺更是达到炉火纯青的境界。

• 御墨（清）
Ink for royal use (Qing Dynasty, 1644-1911)

清末，制墨工匠谢崧岱、谢崧梁借鉴传统制墨的工艺和配方，创制了使用方便、易储存的液体墨汁，并在北京开设了专营墨汁的作坊"一得阁"。液体墨汁的创制是墨史上的又一次革新，给中国书画艺术带来了新的生机。

sell their signature product innovated from a traditional formula. Their ink liquid was easy to use and to store—no grinding was needed. As another milestone made in Chinese history, this invention brought a brand new look to Chinese painting and calligraphy.

清代徽墨四大家

The Best Known Four *Hui* Style Makers During the Qing Dynasty

曹素功

清代徽墨四大制墨名家之首。他早年因科举失意而返乡以制墨为业，最初借用制模名家吴叔大的墨模和墨名起家，后来技艺日渐精良，名声远扬，墨业兴旺。曹素功制墨技术冠绝当时，常为权贵和名流定版制墨，最有名的代表作是"紫玉光墨"。他还善制仿古墨，仿制了从汉代到明代的各种名墨，有"天下之墨推歙州，歙州之墨推曹氏"的美誉。曹素功还著有《墨林》两卷，主要辑录珍品墨和墨客题咏，是难得的墨史资料。他所开设的"艺粟斋"墨庄，子孙相传，历经十几代，绵延三百多年，最后发展为近代著名的上海墨厂。

Cao Sugong

As the great master who topped the four, he entered this business in his hometown after he was seriously frustrated in seeking officialdom by attending royal examinations. He began with the moulds from his famous uncle but his excellent skill quickly spread his own name across the country. The rich and powerful scrambled for customer-tailored products. Of all of his works the most famous was "purple jade and shining ink". He was a master hand in imitation of ancient products, able to make replicas of everything from the Han to the Ming Dynasties. His legendary skill won him a tremendous reputation. He left two volumes of writing, which documented precious varieties of ink and poems and essays related to it. The two volumes of his made a valuable source for tracing the ink making history. He also left a retail business, which, after the management of generations over the past three hundred years, developed into the famous Shanghai Ink Plant in modern China.

- 仿曹素功制集锦墨（清）

  Imitation of Cao Sugong's ink set (Qing Dynasty, 1644-1911)

- 清代汪近圣制集锦墨

  Ink set made by Wang Jinsheng (Qing Dynasty, 1644-1911)

汪近圣

清代徽墨四大家之一。他原本是曹素功"艺粟斋"的墨工，后来离开曹家，在徽州府城自立门户，开设"鉴古斋"墨店。汪近圣在徽墨中独树一帜，其所制之墨雕刻精细，装饰奇巧，艺术价值极高。汪近圣制墨，以小墨见长，著名的"黄山墨"、"新安山水"、"千秋光"等墨为其代表作。

Wang Jinsheng

Another one in the famous four, Wang Jinsheng had worked for Cao Sugong but later left to establish his own business under the name of *Jian Gu Zhai* in Huizhou. His products featured painstaking efforts made in inscriptions and ornamentation and because of this his works possessed an unusual value of art. Most of his products were small, the best known being "Mount Huang" "Scenes of Xin'an" "Light of Thousand Years" and others.

汪节庵

清代徽墨四大家之一，歙派最后一位代表人物。汪节庵制墨秉承徽州传统工艺流程，精选原料，改良技艺，所制之墨十分畅销。他创立了"函璞斋"，与曹素功"艺粟斋"、汪近圣"鉴古斋"并驾齐驱。汪节庵制作的墨有独特的香味，以"烟香自有龙麝气"而著名。汪氏的经典墨品有"兰陵氏书画墨"、"青麟髓墨"、"新安大好山水墨"和集锦墨"西湖图"、"古币墨"等。汪节庵之后，歙派及整个徽州地区的制墨业开始走向衰落。

Wang Jiean

Another one in the famous four, also the last of the *She* School, featuring emphasis on traditional technology, tough material selection and continuous improvement. His store enjoyed an equal reputation as those of other making masters. His products, however, had an unusual fragrance, something described as "heavenly fine". The best known products of his were "Painting and Calligraphy Ink of Lanling" "Landscape in Xin'an" "West Lake" and so on and so forth. After him, the *She* Style, as well as the ink making in Huizhou, declined.

胡开文

清代徽墨休宁派制墨的著名传人，他是清代制墨名家中商业成就最高的。他曾在曹素功墨店做工匠，后开设"胡开文墨庄"。胡开文制墨以集锦墨闻名于世，他精雕墨模，优选材料，其代表作是"苍佩室墨"。胡氏不但注重墨的内在质量，更注重墨模的雕刻和设计，不惜斥巨资搜集名胜古迹的蓝图，还邀请名家、名匠重新绘制雕刻，制出《御园图景》墨64块，墨中的图案包括圆明园、长春园、万春园、北海、中南海等园林景致。在经营上，胡开文非常有远见，他派儿子到全国各地销墨，积极扩大销售范围和影响力，在长江沿岸和东南沿海地区都开设了胡开文分店。1915年，胡氏后人所制的"地球"墨获得巴拿马博览会金奖，胡氏墨业更是驰名中外。

Hu Kaiwen

Famous maker during the Qing Dynasty of the well known *Xiuning* School, having the biggest commercial success among his contemporary fellow makers. After working for Cao Sugong, he left to establish his own business "Hu Kaiwen's". He gave equal emphasis on ink quality and mould decorations. His representative work was "Ink Set for Cangpei Studio". He invited famous artists to paint famous scenes of the royal gardens in Beijing. By their illustrations he made the famous "64 Ink Sticks" to show beautiful scenes in the Summer Palace, Changchun and Wanchun gardens, the Beihai Park and Zhongnanhai, all being the best known in the city. As a shrewd businessman he sent his children out to sell and to increase market shares and influence. He had retail businesses along the Yangtze and all over the southeastern coastal areas. In 1915, the ink stick "Earth" made by one of his descendents won a gold prize on the Panama World Expo. Beginning from this, the fame of his business became international.

- 胡开文套墨（清）

Ink set made by Hu Kaiwen (Qing Dynasty, 1644-1911)

> 墨的种类

墨通常可以按照用材、形制、图绘、用途四种方法划分。

> Varieties of Ink Sticks

Ink can be categorized by materials, shapes, decorative patterns and use.

墨的用材

古代制墨的原料可分为基本原料和配料两类。

基本原料包括色素原料和连接原料。色素原料是将有机物经不完全燃烧，从烟尘中提取无定型炭粉得来的。松烟墨所用色素原料叫"松烟"，是用松树枝干和根烧烟而得。油烟墨所用色素原料叫"油烟"，是用桐油和少量不同比例的动植物油、生漆等烧烟而得。漆烟墨所用色素原料是燃烧漆料而得。连接原料是制造墨的黏合剂，它是墨块成形的主要材料，一般是用动物的皮、骨熬煮而成的动物胶制成，最开始制墨多用鹿胶、麋胶，后来慢慢流行牛皮胶。

制墨的配料是各个名家秘而不宣的独门秘诀。据统计，可用来制墨的配料超过一千种，常用的包括鸡蛋清、鱼皮胶、牛皮胶、各种香料以及各种药材。

● 制墨配料珍珠
Pearl as a kind of material for ink making

Materials

In ancient times, ink materials had two parts, the fundamental and the supplements.

The fundamental included pigments and connectors. Pigments came from the charcoal residues from incompletely burned organic matter. The pigment from burnt pine leaves or roots was called "pine ash", while the pigment from oil was called "oil ash" from tung oil burnt with a percentage of animal fat and raw lacquer. The lacquer soot ink came from burnt lacquer. The connectors meant adhesives, something to solidify ink, usually being glue from boiling animal's bone and fat. The oldest glue used was deer glue or weed glue. Later they were replaced by ox hide clue.

Ingredients for ink making, a top secret to any maker, might be over a thousand but the most common ones being egg white, fish glue, ox glue perfumes and traditional Chinese medicines.

● 制墨原料白芨和胶料
Bletilla and glue for ink making

按用材来分，古墨可以分为松烟墨、油烟墨、油松墨、彩墨、青墨、茶墨、再和墨、药墨、蜡墨等。

松烟墨以松枝或松树树干烧烟制成；油烟墨以桐油、麻油、猪油等烧烟制成；油松墨以油烟和松烟混合制成；洋烟墨以煤或石油烧烟制成；彩墨以五色或十色颜料制成，常用的颜料有朱砂、银朱、雄

By materials ancient ink could be classified into following types: the pine soot, the oil soot, Chinese pine soot, the color, the pale green, the tea, *Zai He* or mixture, the medicine and the wax.

The pine soot ink was made with the ash from burnt pine leaves, the oil soot ink with the residuals from burnt tung oil, sesame oil or lard. Chinese pine soot ink came from the mixture of pine soot

精、赭石、石黄、石青、石绿、蛤粉等；青墨、茶墨以油烟或松烟添加其他色泽原料制成，墨色含黛黑或茶褐色；再和墨以退胶的古墨、陈墨捣碎后再掺入新的色素和连接料重新加工制成；药墨以油烟和阿胶为主要原料，添加入金箔、麝香、牛黄、犀角、羚角、珍珠粉、琥珀、青黛、熊胆、牛胆、蛇胆、猪胆、青鱼胆等制成墨锭，可用于书画，亦可内服或外敷，具有清热、止血、解毒等作用；蜡墨以蜡为黏结材料制成，是拓碑刻专用之物，携带方便。

and oil soot, while the *Yang Yan* type came from the burnt coal or fossil oil. Color ink used materials in five or even ten colors like the cinnabar, vermilion, realgar, ochere… the pale green ink and tea ink had, apart from pine soot or oil soot, pigments from other sources, thus in a pale black color. The *Zai He* type, unlike other varieties, was made with ground old ink sticks with new pigments and connectors. Medicinal ink took oil soot and donkey-hide gelatin as chief materials plus gold foil, musk, bezoar, rhinoceros horn, antelope horn… This variety, beside for painting, was taken as a medicine to lower excessive heat, stop bleeding and remove toxic stuff from body. Wax ink, as its name suggested, had much wax in it. It was a special tool to make rubbings off stone inscriptions, a variety very easy to be carried along.

● 乾隆款朱砂墨（清）
Cinnabar ink, Qian Long Style, (Qing Dynasty, 1644-1911)

按墨的形制可以分为圆形墨、正方形墨、长方形墨、多边形墨和杂佩墨。其中杂佩墨是指模仿古代玉器、花草虫鱼、人物器具的形制所制的墨。

By shape, ink sticks can be classified in to round, square, rectangular, multiple-sided and the irregular, which meant fashioned after a flower, grass, insect, fish, human figure or famous jade object from history.

• 圆形墨、圭形墨
Round ink stick; jade-tablet ink stick

"图绘"是指墨锭身上的装饰图案。按墨身上的图绘名目,明朝制墨名家方于鲁将墨分为六种:与皇帝有关的称"国宝",与国家精粹有关的称"国华",与神话有关的称"博古",与人类生活有关的称"博物",与佛教有关的称"大莫",与老子、庄子有关的称"太玄"。

按用途不同,墨还可以分为贡墨、御墨、文人自制墨、礼品墨、仿古墨、集锦墨等几种。

Tu hui or decorations, referred to a painting or inscription printed or inscribed onto ink sticks. Ming-dynasty ink maker Fang Yulu classified ink sticks into six types by *Tu hui*: "state treasure" for those related to emperors, "national treasure" for those related to the people, "antiques" for those related to mythology, "miscellaneous things" for those related to daily life, "great way" for those related to Buddhism and "supreme" for those related to Laozi and Zhuangzi.

● 十六罗汉图墨（清）

Ink sticks of the sixteen Buddhist guardians(Qing Dynasty, 1644-1911)

贡墨是古代地方官以进贡方式为宫廷生产的专用墨；御墨是皇帝专用的墨；文人自制墨是文人向制墨者定制的墨，在墨种、形制、图案、铭文上都可遂自己的意愿；礼品墨是制墨者出于商业目的而制作的墨，主要用于欣赏、送礼、收藏；仿古墨是用传世的古墨模制作的新墨，作陈设、观赏、收藏、馈赠用；套墨是两锭以上装成一盒的墨；集锦墨是套墨中的一种，为明代制墨名家汪中山所创，盛行于清

By use, ink can also be classified into tributes for emperors, for the royal use only, ink made by scholars, gift ink, imitated antique ink and ink set.

The tributes were made by local officials for the emperor while for the royal use only was the order placed by the emperor. Ink made by scholars was customer-tailored in a specified variety, shape and decorative pattern. Gift ink meant a present given for a commercial purpose, mainly for display, collection or appreciation rather than for a writing purpose. Ink set was a packaged set usually

● 金光悌进贡墨（清）
Tribute ink sticks from Jin Guangti (Qing Dynasty, 1644-1911)

代，其特点是在一个主题下，设计出形制多样、装饰图案不同，但内容上又有联系的几十锭墨，组成一套，放在一盒里。

having more than one stick. The assorted ink, a type of ink set, was an invention by Ming-dynasty Wang Zhongshan, but didn't become a fashion until the following Qing Dynasty. It featured different but associated patterns out of the same subject matter, usually up to dozens of ink sticks packaged in the same box.

• 胡开文制集锦墨（清）
Assorted ink sticks Hu Kaiwen made (Qing Dynasty, 1644-1911)

> 墨的收藏

中国古墨品种很多，在墨史上使用较多、地位较高的主要是松烟墨、油烟墨两种。另外，制墨名地徽州所产的徽墨也是墨史上重要的墨品，制墨名家大多也来自此地，他们制作的许多精美绝伦的墨，是墨收藏的主要对象。

徽墨

徽墨是中国古墨中最有名的墨品，因产于古徽州府而得名。现在的黄山市屯溪区、绩溪县、歙县等地为古代徽墨的制造中心。徽墨的创始人是南唐制墨名家奚超及其子奚廷珪（李廷珪），徽墨历史已逾千年。

徽墨品种繁多，传统品种有漆烟墨、油烟墨、松烟墨、全烟墨、

> Ink Collection

Of all varieties, pine soot and oil soot inks were more used in history, thus more collectable than other kinds. So is the ink made in Huizhou for its unique position in history and many famous makers related to it. Many ink sticks they made are valuable to collectors.

The *Hui* Style Ink

As the best known variety, it got its name from the place it was made, Huizhou covering today's Tunxi, Jixi and the Shexian County, all being active in ink business in ancient times. *Hui* style ink was invented by the Southern Tang maker Xi Chao and his son, Xi Tinggui (also named Li Tinggui). By now, this style is over a thousand years old.

Even this variety has many types in it: lacquer soot, oil soot, pine soot,

净烟墨、减胶墨、加香墨等。现代徽墨在传统工艺的基础上不断创新，改良了茶墨、青墨、朱砂墨、五彩墨和手卷墨等品种，并开发了许多新品种，同时恢复了一些古代名品。

徽墨具有色泽黑润、历久不褪、入纸如晕、舐笔不胶、润泽生光、馨香浓郁、防腐防蛀、造型美观、装饰典雅等特点，深得历代书画家的喜爱。徽墨以松烟、桐油烟、漆烟、胶为主要原料，掺入二十多种其他原料精制而成。徽墨集绘画、书法、雕刻、造型等艺术于一体，使墨本身成为一种综合性的艺术珍品。

在徽墨发展的过程中，形成了歙县墨、休宁墨、婺源墨三大流派。三大流派各具特色，争奇斗

all soot, pure soot, reduced glue and increased glue. Modern types are innovated from traditional technology: the tea, the pale black, the cinnabar, the five colors and the hand roll. Some varieties that lost in history are brought back to life.

The *Hui* style ink gives a very pleasant look, jet black, glossy and a dream-like effect on paper. It never glues the tip together. Also, it gives a fragrant smell, able to withstand inspects and highly decorative. For these features the *Hui* style ink has been a favor to artists throughout history. It takes pine soot, tung oil soot, lacquer soot and glue as chief materials plus twenty some supplements. *Hui* style ink sticks, in themselves, are works of art with charm of painting, calligraphy, carving, sculpturing and modeling.

The *Hui* style ink has three varieties, the Shexian variety, the Xiuning variety and Wuyuan variety, each highlights ink culture from a different perspective. The Shexian variety features an antique look, very fine in texture with very clear glue in

• 耕织图墨（清）
Ink sticks in farming and weaving motif
(Qing Dynasty, 1644-1911)

艳，极大地丰富和发展了中国的墨文化，为中华文化的发展作出了贡献。歙县墨的特点是仿古隽雅，烟细胶清，多为贡墨及名家托造墨，以罗小华、程君房、方于鲁、潘一驹、曹素功为代表人物。休宁墨的特点是绚丽精致，饰金髹彩，多为套墨，尤其是集锦墨得到当时统治阶级及文房用品收藏爱好者的钟爱，以汪中山、叶玄卿、邵格之、吴天章为代表。婺源墨的特点是朴实少纹，具有典型的民间艺术风格，深受人们的欢迎，以詹云鹏、詹衡襄、詹致、詹成圭和詹子云等为代表人物。

it, often used as tributes for emperors and gifts customer tailed by celebrities. This variety had big names like Luo Xiaohua, Cheng Junfang, Fang Yulu, Pan Yiju and Cao Sugong. The Xiuning variety presents a very luxurious look in gold or silver, often appearing as a set much favored by the rich and powerful and sought after by collectors. This variety also had big names, Wang Zhongshan, Ye Xuanqing, Shao Gezhi and Wu Tianzhang to name a few. The Wu Yuan variety had less decoration on it but was more antique looking, much preferred by people of higher taste. This variety has Zhan Yunpeng, Zhan Hengxiang and Zhan Zhi, etc, as representatives.

具有收藏价值的墨

现在存世的古墨已十分稀少，保存完好的古墨更是少有，因此古墨收藏越来越受到人们的青睐。具有增值价值的古墨多是出自名家之手的作品，目前存世较多的是明清时期的古墨。其中做工精细，品质优良，保存完好的宫廷御墨是最值得收藏的一个品种。

一般说来，实用墨的收藏价值远低于观赏墨，因为观赏墨的墨模多是雕刻名家精心所作，墨的图绘精美异常，具有很高的艺术价值。

品质优良的古墨经过千锤百炼，虽历千年但不会变质。通常说来，质地细腻、坚硬难化、胶量适中、墨色亮泽、清香弥久是优质古墨必备的要素。

Collectable Ink Sticks

Ancient ink sticks that have survived history are few and complete ones even fewer. So they are much sought after by many people. Of all, those from famous makers have more added values. Of all ancient sticks we see today, most come from the Ming and the Qing Dynasties. Those for royal use only, made with the best craftsmanship and still in good condition are hot to collectors.

Usually, ink for practical use is less valuable than the ink for appreciation because the later often came from moulds having been made by famous artists with artistic decoration.

A nice antique ink stick will last for a thousand years without going bad. Such an ink stick often features fine texture, solid, hard and difficult to dissolve, having glossy looks and a pleasant smell.

• 富贵图墨（清）

Ink sticks in wealth and rank motif
(Qing Dynasty, 1644-1911)

墨的保养

墨无论是松烟墨，还是油烟墨，都是用胶黏合在一起的，因此既怕受潮霉烂，又怕干燥爆裂。所以，防潮、防干燥是长期保存古墨最重要的两点。刚收藏的墨，应用纸包起来封好，平放在盒子中，再将墨盒挂于通风阴凉处，避免墨与潮湿空气直接接触。

如果古墨存放不当，很可能出现受潮、断裂、弯曲等问题，这时就需要对其进行保养。保养古墨通常选择在最干燥的季节。以手抚墨，用汗气润泽它，如果常将古墨揣在身上，受些人气，可保持较好的干湿度。

对于已严重受潮、生霉斑的古墨，不要急于除霉斑，应当先去湿。具体方法是先用绵纸将墨锭包封好，放置在生石灰中，过十余天取出，墨中的潮气便会去掉。再用软毛刷子或软纸擦去霉斑。

断裂的古墨可以用磨的浓墨做黏合剂，将断块黏合起来。

墨锭变弯曲可能是因为放置方法不正确造成的，不能用力扳、压、敲墨锭。正确的补救方法是用纸把墨包封好，将弯突的一方向上，平放好，在上面压上一本不太重的书，过些日子再加重，时日一久，墨就会矫正过来。

The Keeping of Ink Sticks

Both the pine soot and oil soot ink sticks have glue in it and because of the glue they easily go moldy and are likely affected with damp. They may also crack from excessive dryness. Keeping them from damp and dryness is crucial. A new ink stick should be wrapped in paper before placed flat inside a box in a shady and ventilated place. This is to keep the ink out of a direct contact with wet air.

Left in a poor condition antique ink sticks may get affected with damp, break or warp. If this happens repairing is necessary, often done in a dry season. Stroking it with hand to moisten it with sweat. Carrying it along in one's body also helps.

Heavily moldy ones have to get rid of wet before mildew to be removed. The right way is to wrap the ink in tissue paper before left in lime for ten days. By then, humidity is gone. Using very soft brushes or tissue paper to wipe off the mildew.

Broken pieces can be glued back together with thick ink juice.

A warped ink stick may come from incorrect placing. No force should be applied to correction either by pressing, bending or knocking. The correct way is to wrap it with paper and leave it flat with the bending side on top, put some weight, say a book, something not too heavy, on it and after days increase the weight. After a period of time the warp will be gone.

● 名花十友墨（清）
Ink sticks of ten close flower friends (Qing Dynasty, 1644-1911)

纸
Paper

　　文房四宝中的"纸"是指书画用纸，即宜用毛笔写字或作画的纸。造纸术与火药、指南针、印刷术合称为中国古代科学技术的四大发明，为人类文明的传播做出了巨大的贡献。纸的出现，不仅使人们拥有了轻巧方便的书写材料，更成就了中国传统书画艺术。在中国造纸历史中，也产生了许多精美的加工纸，具有极高的观赏价值和艺术价值。

Paper here refers to the paper on which calligraphy or painting or writing is done with a writing brush. Paper making, together with gun powder, compass and printing are called "the four significant inventions the Chinese nation made in ancient history". Paper making made a huge contribution to the spreading of human civilization. As a writing material in light weight and easy to be carried along, paper parented Chinese painting and calligraphy. Apart from the paper for practical need some with high artistic value was invented for appreciation.

> 纸的历史

纸虽然是文房四宝中出现最晚的，但是它为中国传统书画艺术带来的翻天覆地的变化，是其余三宝无法企及的。纸在几千年的发展历程中，不断改进技术，推陈出新，出现了一批又一批各具特色的产品，其中不乏具有较高的艺术价值的精美纸笺。

纸的发明

中国历来就有蔡伦造纸的说法。据《后汉书》记载，东汉元兴元年（105），当时负责制造宫廷御用器具的官员蔡伦，经过潜心研究，发明了造纸术，生产出新的书写材料"蔡侯纸"。但是考古发现表明，纸的诞生远早于蔡伦生活的年代，所以现代学者认为蔡伦只是造纸术的改良者。

> History of Paper

Though being the latest to appear among the four treasures of the study, paper made a change on painting and calligraphy unmatched by any other. During its several thousand years of history, with its making technology improved time and gain, new varieties appeared some being just works of art.

• 蔡伦像
Cai Lun

在纸产生之前，人们所使用的书写材料是竹简和绢帛。竹简是将若干竹片或木片用绳穿系而成，无论是书写、阅读还是搬运，都十分笨重；而绢帛则非常珍贵，无法普及。从考古出土的资料来看，纸应该诞生于秦汉时期。1957年在陕西西安东郊灞桥附近的一座西汉墓中，出土了一批"灞桥纸"。这些纸制作于西汉武帝时期，纤维束较

● **竹简（秦）**

竹简是由竹片或木片穿系而成，体积大，在纸出现之前是主要的书写材料。

Bamboo slips (Qin Dynasty, 221 B.C.-206 B.C.)

Bamboo slips include wood slips for writing purpose. Wood or bamboo, they are bulky. Before the invention of paper they were a major writing material.

Invention of Paper

Paper making is an invention credited to Cai Lun. By *Hou Han Shu* or *History of Late Han*, in the first year of Yuanxing, the Easten Han Dynasty (105), civil official Cai Lun in charge of the supplies for the royal family invented paper making and the paper he made was named Cai Lun paper. However, archeological finds challenged this saying, suggesting paper making was much earlier than Cai Lun's time. Cai Lun, to some contemporary scholars, simply improved the technology.

People wrote on silk or bamboo slips before paper was invented. Bamboo slips were slips bound by a thread, very cumbersome for either transportation or using, while silk was expensive, beyond many people's means. From archeological finds paper making should have happened during the Qin or the Han Dynasties (221 B.C.-220 A.D.). In 1957, archeologists unearthed some paper from a Western Han tomb on the eastern suburb of Xi'an. That paper in a pale yellowish color, called Baqiao paper, was made during the Emperor Wu's time and contained fiber in disarray. It was exclusively used for rapping burial objects. Later, in Gansu,

多，交织不匀，呈浅黄色，专门用来包裹陪葬物品。后来甘肃省境内又陆续出土了"马圈湾纸"、"放马滩纸"。经考证，这些古纸的时间比"蔡侯纸"早了100～300年。

more ancient paper called by historians as Majuanwan and Fangmatan paper was discovered. Studies have proved they were earlier than Cai Lun's time by 100 to 300 years.

- 帛书（汉）

绢帛是丝织品，成本高，在纸出现之前是珍贵的书写材料。

Silk book (Han Dynasty, 206 B.C.-220 A.D.)

Silk as an expensive stuff was used for writing before paper was invented.

早期纸的制作以麻为主要原料，制浆主要用石灰水，所制的纸颜色蜡黄，质量不高。经蔡伦改进

Paper was made from hemp in early days, which was pulped by lime water and this explained why paper so made was yellowish and in small quantity.

- 早期写有汉字的纸（汉）

造纸术在东汉时有了技术突破，但在发展初期并没有完全取代竹简和绢帛，而是有一个纸简并存的过渡时期。

Paper with written characters (Han Dynasty, 206 B.C.-220 A.D.)

Although a breakthrough was made during the Eastern Han Dynasty, paper was not enough to replace expensive stuff like silk or cumbersome bamboo slips. For a period of history they co-existed.

后的纸以树皮、碎布、麻头、旧渔网为原料，经过细致的加工，生产出来的纸颜色较白，质地坚韧。蔡伦虽不是纸的制造者，但是对纸的改进做出了卓越的贡献，完成了造纸术的改革和飞跃，为以后雕版印刷用纸创造了物质条件。

After Cai Lun's improvement the range of materials became wider, tree bark, cloth or hemp bits even used fishing net. After being processed by an improved technology the paper made was whiter and stronger than before. Though Cai Lun was not the inventor, he was a significant improver by revolutionizing the making technology, which made a necessary condition for the later paper engraving needed.

蔡伦造纸术

在蔡伦之前，纸的制作技术粗糙，经过蔡伦的改良后，造纸术得到广泛推广，并制造出质量更好的纸。

蔡伦改进造纸术后造纸的基本过程是：把渔网、麻头、破布、树皮等原料先用水浸，然后用斧头切碎，用水洗涤，再用草木灰水浸透并加以蒸煮，然后用清水漂洗后捣碎，再用水配成纸浆，用纸模过滤纸浆，再经过脱水、干燥、抄纸等工序，纸就制造出来了。

蔡伦造纸术相比之前的造纸有了三大进步：一是造纸原料来源拓宽；二是造纸过程增加，分工更细致；三是用草木灰水取代石灰水，草木灰水碱性更强，造出的纸颜色更白。

Cai Lun's Paper Making Technology

Before Cai Lun, the technology to make paper was coarse. After he improved it, the paper made was in a much better quality.

The improved workflow was this: first, soak old fishing net, bits of hemp and cloth and tree bark with water, cut them into very small pieces with axes, wash them before soak them again but this time, with plant ash water; steam them, rinse them clean, pound them into a pulp with water added, filter with a paper mould, then, after dehydration, drying and peeling, paper was made.

This improved technology, if compared with previous one, had three major advantages: a wider range of material source, more steps added to make the procedure more professional and more specific, replacing the lime water with plant ash water, which contained more alkalinity to make the paper whiter.

《天工开物》中的造纸图 宋应星（明）

Paper Making, *Tian Gong Kai Wu* or *The Exploitation of the Works of Nature*, by Song Yingxing (Ming Dynasty, 1368-1644)

造纸术的传播

造纸术首先传入与我国毗邻的朝鲜和越南，之后由朝鲜传到了日本。西晋（265—316）时，越南人就掌握了造纸技术。4世纪时的百济、高句丽、新罗都掌握了造纸术。中国的造纸技术也传播到了中亚的一些国家，并通过贸易传播到了印度。

唐朝（618—907）时，与海外的频繁交往使造纸术传入阿拉伯，到10世纪造纸技术又传到了叙利亚、埃及与摩洛哥。

欧洲人是通过阿拉伯人了解造纸技术的。12世纪，阿拉伯人在西班牙建立了欧洲第一个造纸场。1276年，意大利第一家造纸场建成。14世纪，法国建立造纸场，当时法国造纸不仅供应本国，还向德国出口。14世纪末，德国掌握了造纸术。15世纪英国建立了自己的造纸厂。到了17世纪，欧洲主要国家都掌握了造纸术。

新航线开辟后，西班牙人将造纸术带到美洲。墨西哥造纸始于16世纪。美国在17世纪建立了第一家造纸厂。到19世纪，中国的造纸术已传遍世界五大洲。

Spreading of the Paper Making Technology

First, it spread to the DPR korea and Vietnam, then, via the DPR Korea to Japan. By China's Western Jin Dynasty (265-316), Vietnamese knew how to make paper. Later, during the fourth century A.D. small countries in the states in Korean Peninsula knew it too. Paper making went to central Asia and India through trading activities.

During the Tang Dynasty (618-907), contacts with foreign nations increased, which brought paper making technology to Arab, then, during the tenth century, to Syria, Egypt and Morocco.

Europeans learnt this technology through Arabians. During the 12th century Arabians set up in Spain the first paper making mill Europeans ever had in history. In 1276 Italians had their first. France had theirs during the 14th century. The paper it made was even exported to Germany, who learnt this technique in late 14th century. The British had their paper mill in the 15th century and by the 17th century, all major European countries had theirs.

After the navigation route to America was opened, Spanish people brought this technology to America. Mexico began to make paper during the 16th century, and the Unites States, the 17th century. By the 19th century, paper making technology from China was seen all over the world.

魏晋南北朝时期的纸

魏晋南北朝时期，竹简、绢帛退出历史舞台，纸正式成为主要的书写材料。与汉代相比，魏晋南北朝的纸产地范围更广，产量大幅度提高，造纸技术也进一步提升。制纸中心从河南洛阳向全国扩展，形成了南北遍布的新格局，一些边远的少数民族地区也建立起了纸坊，发展造纸业。

魏晋南北朝时期的纸的品种也不断丰富，左伯纸、麻纸、黄麻纸、藤纸、银光纸是这一时期的著名纸品。

- 麻纸《平复贴》【局部】陆机（晋）
Ping Fu Tie, (detail) calligraphic work on hemp paper, by Lu Ji, (Jin Dynasty, 265-420)

The Paper Made During the Wei, Jin and the Southern and Northern Periods

Bamboo slips and silk for writing were replaced by paper during the Wei, Jin and the Southern and Northern Periods (220-589). Unlike the Han Dynasty (206 B.C.-220 A.D.), more places were making paper, the quantity produced was bigger and the technology better. Luoyang of Henan, the old paper making center, saw other centers rising across the country, even in remote areas where ethnic minorities lived.

Also, the varieties of paper became more, *Zuobo*, hemp, yellow hemp, cane and *Yin Guang* or "silver light" being famous kinds.

Zuobo paper came from its inventor Zuo Bo who lived in present-day Laizhou of Shandong Province. During the Three-kingdom Period (220-280) this place was called Donglai. On the basis of traditional technology, by borrowing the experience from Cai Lun, he was able to make very neat and very glossy paper perfect for writing. Scholars then rushed for it.

Hemp paper took hemp fiber as the chief material. It is white and water fast, an ideal material for writing. The famous

左伯纸是三国时期曹魏东莱（今山东莱州）人左伯所制。左伯是当时有名的学者和书法家，他总结历代造纸技艺，借鉴蔡伦造纸的经验，制造出光亮整洁，适于书写用的纸，深受当时文人的欢迎。

麻纸以大麻纤维为主要原料制成，纸质坚韧洁白，耐水浸泡，是理想的书写用纸。东晋著名书法家王羲之、王献之父子常用麻纸练习书法。

黄麻纸是东晋时期在麻纸的基础上研发出的新纸品，也叫"潢纸"。其制作工艺是将麻纸用黄檗汁浸泡，晾干后使用。整个过程被称为"入潢"，经过"入潢"后的黄麻纸，具有防虫蛀蚀的功能。黄麻纸不仅为文人所用，官府文书也常以此纸书写。

藤纸因其主要生产原料为野生藤皮而得名，非常适合书画。这种纸直到唐代仍然为书画家所喜爱。

- 藤纸《快雪时晴帖》【局部】
  王羲之（晋）

  Kuai Xue Shi Qing Tie, or *Calligraphic Work after Snow*, calligraphic work on cane paper by Wang Xizhi (Jin Dynasty, 265-420)

father and son calligraphers, Wang Xizhi and Wang Xianzhi during the Eastern Jin Dynasty, used this paper for practice.

Yellow hemp paper was developed from hemp paper, a variety also called *Huang Zhi*. It was made with hemp paper after soaked through by cork tree water and drying up. This process was called "into the cork tree bark". After this process, paper was insect proof, used by scholars and officials alike.

Cane paper got its name from rattan, very good for calligraphic and painting

銀光纸产于安徽黟县、歙县一带，纸质光润洁白，采用表面涂布的加工技术，在纸面糊上白色矿物细粉并予以研光。这种纸的制造，为此后宣纸的出现奠定了工艺基础。

隋唐五代时期的纸

隋唐五代时期，社会文化空前繁荣，文化艺术的兴盛带动了造纸业的发展。

这一时期造纸原料以树皮为主，常见的有楮皮、桑皮，也掺杂其他带有香味的树皮，所制之纸称为"皮纸"。皮纸柔中带劲，纤维交错均匀，易于保存。

此时纸的加工技术在前代的基础之上有很大提高，涂蜡、施胶等新工艺的运用，使纸更加润滑、光洁。其中以硬黄纸较为著名，它是在潢纸的基础上，再在纸上涂蜡，使纸具有莹润的光泽，质地坚韧，透明性强，书写时运笔流利，可久藏，多用于写经和摹写古帖。

除硬黄纸外，这一时期的名贵纸品还有水纹纸、薛涛笺、澄心堂纸、高丽纸等。

水纹纸是唐代名纸品，其制造

art. Even by the Tang Dynasty this variety was still in favor.

Yin Guang or the "Silver Light" came from Yixian and Shexian counties of Anhui Province. This variety features a very white and shining surface coming from coating with shining white mineral particles. The appearance of this paper laid foundation for the birth of *Xuan* paper in later years.

Paper Made During the Sui, the Tang and the Five-dynasty Periods

Culture gained a big progress during the Sui, the Tang and the Five-dynasty Periods (581-960) and art activities were booming, which helped the progress of paper making.

However, the chief materials for paper making during these periods of history were barks from mulberry and other kinds with fragrance. The paper made with tree barks was called *Pi Zhi*, meaning it was tough with disarrayed fiber in it. This variety could be kept for a long time.

The technology was much improved and something new happened like wax coating and glue application to make paper smooth and shiny. The hard yellow paper was the best known, made from

工艺特殊，将纸逐幅在刻有字画的文版上碾磨，或用刻有纹理、图案的模子置于纸面进行碾磨，纸面上便隐起各种花纹图案，放在迎光处可显现透亮的线纹图案。此种纸多用作信纸、诗笺、书法帖纸。

• 水纹纸《张翰帖》【局部】欧阳询（唐）
Zhang Han Tie, (detail) calligraphic work on water wave paper by Ouyang Xun (Tang Dynasty, 618-907)

薛涛笺是唐末五代名笺纸，因由女诗人薛涛创制而得名。薛涛笺是一种加工染色纸，属于红色小幅诗笺，其特点是省料、加工方便、生产成本低。

the Huang paper plus a coat of wax to make it tough, shiny, harder and more transparent. It gave a fluent writing on it, also, could be kept longer than other kinds. This variety was often used for Buddhist sutra writing or copying of ancient calligraphy works.

Other famous varieties during these periods were water waves, Xue Tao, *Cheng Xin Tang* and the Korean, named either after their inventor, a famous literary man or its birthplace.

Water Wave was a famous kind during the Tang Dynasty. It came from a very special making process: carving the pattern or characters onto a plate, rubbing this paper against a the plate until it picked it up. Against light this paper showed a beautiful pattern on the surface. It was a very romantic material for letters, poetry writing or calligraphic works.

Xue Tao paper, a dyed paper popular in the late Tang (618-907) and the Five-dynasty Period (907-960) that followed got its name from famous female poet Xue Tao. It was often red and in a small size for writing an improvised poem, a paper of less cost and easy to make.

笺纸

笺纸又称"花笺"、"诗笺"、"彩笺"、"尺牍"，是供人写信作诗用的小张书画纸，产生于南北朝时期，当时称"八行笺"。从唐宋开始一直到明清，笺纸都十分流行，比较有名的有薛涛笺、谢公笺等。

另外，还有一种印有诗文图画的信笺，属于工艺用纸，叫做"笺谱"。最具代表性的名笺谱是明代的《十竹斋笺谱》、《萝轩变古笺谱》。笺谱由于所绘图画大都出于名家之手而具有较高的收藏价值和艺术价值。

● 笺纸 金冬心手札（清）
Jin Dongxin's calligraphy on letter paper
(Qing Dynasty, 1644-1911)

Letter Paper

This variety had other names, flower paper, poetry paper, color paper… it was for the writing of a small size calligraphic work or painting or writing a letter or a poem. The first time it appeared was the Southern and Northern Dynasties under the name of "eight line paper". It was popular during the Tang, the Song Dynasties and down to the Ming and the Qing Dynasties. Famous styles in this variety were Xue Tao and Lord Xie papers.

Jianpu was a kind with printed poems or painting on it. The most representative form of this kind was the Ming-dynasty *Shi Zhu Zhai* and *Luo Xuan Bian Gu*. The paintings they carried were often the prints of works by renowned artists. Because of this, this variety was highly collectable and artistically valuable.

● 笺谱（清）
Jianpu paper (Qing Dynasty, 1644-1911)

澄心堂纸是徽州地区所产的一种宣纸，是南唐后主李煜命人专为宫廷所制。此纸以楮树皮为主要原料，纸质柔韧细腻，光滑吸墨，因李煜将此纸藏于自己读书批奏章的处所澄心堂内而得名。后世视澄心堂纸为艺术珍品，存世者极为稀少。

Cheng Xin Tang was a *Xuan* paper from Huizhou, said to have been made for royal use only by the instruction of Li Yu, ruler of the Southern Tang Dynasty. This variety has a very fine texture, glossy and very good at absorbing ink. Because Li Yu kept it inside his study *Cheng Xin Tang*, it got its name. To later generations, this paper was priceless, very little to have come down in history.

• 《澄心堂纸帖》蔡襄（宋）
Cheng Xin Tang Zhi Tie, by Cai Xiang (Song Dynasty, 960-1279)

梅尧臣得纸赋诗

梅尧臣（1002—1060），北宋著名的现实主义诗人。他每次得到佳纸必赋诗，以此表达心中的激动欣喜。一次，梅尧臣的挚友欧阳修得到十张宫内的澄心堂纸，赠予梅尧臣数张"佳物共享"。梅尧臣得纸后，激动不已，写下《永叔寄澄心堂纸二幅》。

Poem Composed by Mei Yaochen after He Received *Cheng Xin Tang* paper

Mei Yaochen (1002-1060), poet of realism school during the Northern Song Dynasty (1127-1279), was said to compose a poem each time he received a rare variety of paper. Once, after he received a couple of sheets of *Cheng Xin Tang* paper as a gift from his close friend Ouyang Xiu, who had received ten from somewhere, Mei Yaochen was so excited that he wrote a famous poem titled "*Upon the Receipt of Two Sheets of Cheng Xin Tang Paper*".

• 梅尧臣像
Mei Yaochen

纸是古代高丽国向唐朝进贡的贡品。古籍《负暄野录》中记载了这种纸的特点："高丽纸以棉、茧造成，色白如绫，坚韧如帛，用以书写，发墨可爱。此中国所无，亦奇品也。"此纸多为粗条帘纹，纸纹距大且厚于白皮纸，仅吸收水分而不易吸墨。

Korean paper was a tribute to Tang emperors from Korea. By *Fu Xuan Ye Lu* or *Unofficial Records of Anecdotes*, "this variety of paper was made with cotton or silk, as white as brocade, able to give a pleasant look when applied with ink. It was not native in China, but something from another country." This paper had bold veins and thicker than white leather paper. It absorbed water, not ink.

宣纸

宣纸是中国古代造纸业中重要的纸类，它从唐代开始便是中国社会的主流用纸，在文化传承中起到了重要的作用。

宣纸因产于宣州而得名，其原料有檀树皮、楮树皮、桑树皮、竹、麻等数十种。相传宣纸是蔡伦的后世弟子孔丹在晋代创制。一次，孔丹在河边发现了一棵老檀树倒在河水里。经过河水浸泡，檀树皮的纤维被漂白，孔丹取其纤维制纸，宣纸由此而成。

宣纸洁白如玉、绵韧而坚、柔软均匀。这种纸利于书画，润墨性强，墨晕层次分明。另外它还有耐老化、防虫蛀、耐热、耐光的性能，适合长期保存，有"千年美纸"、"纸中之王"的美称。宣纸被大量运用于书画领域，而且被推广到木版水印、装潢裱托、拓片印刷以及贵重档案资料保存等方面。

宣纸按加工方法的不同，可分为生宣、熟宣、半熟宣三种。生宣是没有经过额外加工的宣纸，吸水性和沁水性都强，水墨渗沁迅速，易产生丰富的墨韵变化，多用于绘制泼墨画和写意山水画。熟宣是宣纸加工时涂以明矾，纸质比生宣硬，吸水能力弱，使用时墨和颜料不会洇散开来，但久藏会出现漏矾和脆裂的现象，多用于绘制工笔画和书写楷书、隶书。半熟宣是用生宣浸以各种植物汁液而成，具有微弱的抗水力。其特点是较熟宣易吸水，又不似生宣那样容易化水，主要适

● **宣纸（现代）**
Xuan paper (contemporary product)

● **五牛图 韩滉（唐）**
宣纸适合长期保存，这幅《五牛图》历经千余年仍然保持着原画的风貌。
Five Oxen, by Han Huang (Tang Dynasty, 618-907)
Xuan paper is almost ageless. This painting, after a thousand years, is still in good shape.

用于书写小幅屏条、册页或用作兼工带写的绘画。

另外，宣纸按用料不同，又可分为棉料、净皮、特净三类。棉料是指原材料檀皮含量在40％左右的纸，较薄、较轻；净皮是指檀皮含量达到60％以上的；而特净是原材料檀皮的含量达到80％以上。皮料成分越重，纸张越能经受拉力，质量也越好，更能体现丰富的墨迹层次和润墨效果，越能经受笔力，并且反复搓揉而纸面不会破。

每种宣纸又有单宣、夹宣、二层、三层之分，规格上有四尺、六尺、八尺、丈二、丈四、丈八等区别。

- 半熟宣书法（清）
Calligraphy on "the medium" *Xuan* paper (Qing Dynasty, 1644-1911)

Xuan Paper

An important kind of paper made in ancient China, ever since its birth the *Xuan* paper made chief means for writing in society, very important to the progress of Chinese culture.

It got its name from its birthplace Xuanzhou. Among its materials were barks from wingceltis, mulberry, bamboo and hemp…. This variety was said invented by a follower of Cai Lun named Kong Dan during the Jin Dynasty. Once, he saw a wingceltis tree soaked in river water which had bleached its fibers. He tried to make paper with these fibers so the *Xuan* paper was born.

Xuan paper was white, tough and soft, very good for painting and calligraphic writing. It absorbed more ink than any other kind and able to give a dream-like feeling. It withstood aging and threats from insects, heat and light. It could be kept for a long time and

- 宣纸（现代）
Xuan paper (contemporary product)

because of this it was named "paper of thousand years" "king of papers". It was seen in many art forms like woodblock printing, mounting, rubbing and recording of important documents.

By different processing *Xuan* paper can be classified as *Sheng Xuan* or "raw *Xuan*", *Shu Xuan* or "cooked *Xuan*" and *Ban Shu Suan* "the medium". *Sheng Xuan* was *Xuan* paper without additional processing but very hydrophilic; ink applied on it spread quickly to produce a cloud-like look. This type was good for ink-splashing landscape. *Shu Xuan* had alums added, crispy and less hydrophilic, difficult for ink to spread on it. Long storage might have alums leak and paper breaks. This variety was good for *gong-bi* style painting or calligraphy in official and regular scripts. Ban *Shu Xuan* came *Sheng Xuan* paper processed with juice extract from plants. It was less hydrophilic, something between Shu and Sheng kinds. This kind was good for writing small-size hanging scrolls and painting albums with calligraphy to go with.

Xuan paper can also be classified into three types by materials: the cotton, the pure and the purist. The cotton referred to *Xuan* paper with 40 percent of wingceltis bark fiber, often thinner and lighter. The pure referred to 60 percent of wingceltis bark fiber, while the purist, above 80 percent. The more wingceltis fiber it contained the more endurable, tougher and in better quality the paper was, able to show different shades of ink and to withstand rough handling.

Xuan paper has single layer, the lined, two layers and even three layers types. It had different sizes from 4 *chi* per side to 6, 8, 12, 14 even 18 *chi* per side.

宋元时期的纸

宋元时期，造纸术得到进一步发展，印刷术的发明更促进了造纸产业的扩张。

宋元制纸原料就地取材，沿用树皮的同时，还引入竹、麦秆等材料。在盛产竹子的南方制造出洁白柔软、浸润保墨、纤维细腻、绵韧平整的竹纸，深得文人墨客的青睐。

宋代制纸业将前代的砑光、染色等技术加以发挥，发明了金粟笺纸、谢公笺、元书纸、明仁殿纸等名纸。

Paper Made During the Song and the Yuan Dynasties

Paper making further progressed during the Song (960-1279) and the Yuan Dynasties (1279-1368), particularly after the invention of printing.

Paper making during the Song and the Yuan Dynasties took local materials and apart from tree barks included bamboo and wheat stalks. In the south, where bamboo was abundant, very white and very soft bamboo paper was made, good in absorbing ink with a finer texture. This paper was much welcome to scholars and artists.

- 金粟笺纸《二经同卷》（宋）
Buddhist sutra on *Jin Su* paper (Song Dynasty, 960-1279)

金粟笺纸是一种盛产于歙州的以桑皮为原料的纸，因浙江海盐金粟山下的金粟寺用其大量抄写经书而得名。其特点是质地硬密，表面光滑，纤维分布均匀，呈半透明，一面呈浅黄色，一面呈深黄色，防蛀抗水，寿命很长，虽历千年，犹如新制。

谢公笺是一种经过染色加工的纸，为文人谢景初所创，因色彩丰富又名"十色笺"，也就是十种颜色的书写专用纸。这种纸色彩艳丽新颖，雅致有趣，有深红、粉红、杏红、明黄、深青、浅青、深绿、浅绿、铜绿、浅云十种色，在历史上与唐代的薛涛笺齐名。

Song-dynasty paper making took calendaring and coloring a step further. It invented new kinds, many being famous in history.

Jin Su was made with mulberry bark in Shezhou. It got its name from a temple in Zhejiang, which requested a large quantity of *Xuan* paper for copying sutras. This *Jin Su* paper had a strong and closely knitted texture, very fine and smooth with cvenly distributed fiber, transparent to some degree, yellowish on one side and dark yellow on the other, moth and water proof. It had a long life span, even after a thousand years it might still look as good as new.

Lord Xie's letter paper was colored, which got its name from famous

元书纸是一种采用当年生的嫩毛竹作为原料，以手工抄造制成的书写用纸，在北宋真宗时期（998—1022）被选作御用文书纸，因皇帝元祭（元日庙祭）时用以书写祭文而称"元书纸"。其特点是洁白柔韧，微含竹子清香，落水易溶，着墨不渗，久藏不蛀、不变色。

明仁殿纸是元代的一种加工纸，专供宫廷内府使用。明仁殿是皇帝看书的地方，这种纸供皇帝御用，所以叫"明仁殿纸"。由于此纸名贵，在明清时期多有仿制。

scholar Xie Jingchu. Because of bright colors it had it was also called "ten-color paper", which meant "writing paper in ten different colors", equally famous as Xue Tao paper during the Tang.

The *Yuan Shu* writing paper took fresh bamboo as its material. During the Emperor Zhenzong period of the Northern Song Dynasty(998-1022) it was selected as paper for royal use, especially for writing memorial articles to be read on a memorializing ceremony for a diseased emperor. It featured a white color and a very pleasant smell; it easily dissolved in water but difficult for ink to ooze, also mothproof and its color lasting longer.

The *Ming Ren Dian* paper during the Yuan Dynasty (1279-1368) was for royal use only. It got its name from the palace where emperors read and wrote. Because of its tremendous fame its imitations were made in later dynasties of the Ming and the Qing Dynasties.

Changes also happened to the size. During the Song and the Yuan Dynasties a much bigger format than before was made and this marked a big progress. Recycling of used paper began during the Southern Song, which processed the

笔墨纸砚
Writing Brush, Ink Stick, Paper and Ink Slab

宋元时期纸的幅制也有改进，可制造远大于前代的巨幅纸。这是宋代制纸技术进步的重要标志。南宋时期，还开创了对纸的再利用技术，将使用过的纸作为原料，进行制作、加工成为新纸，名为"还魂纸"。这种再造纸是技术成熟的重要表现。

宋代还出现了关于纸的专著——苏易简所著《文房四谱》中的《纸谱》，这是中国最早的制纸专著。宋代雕版印刷术的发展，不但促进了印书业的发展，还带动了制纸业的发展。

used paper into new one. The recycled paper had an interesting name, "back to life" paper. Recycled paper marked the maturity of paper making technology.

Monographs of paper making technology appeared during the Song, as was seen in the *Introductions to paper*, a chapter in *The Four Treasures of the Study* authored by Su Yijian. This chapter was probably the earliest writing about paper making. Also in the Song, engraving came into being, which boosted book printing as well as paper making.

纸与印刷术

中国印刷术是人类文明史上具有划时代意义的发明。它是在笔、墨、纸都具备的物质条件下才创造出来的，其中纸在印刷过程中的作用是无可替代的，是关键的材料。

在印刷之前，需要在纸上先誊写样本，经过校对、上板、刻版等工序，做成上有凸

● 毛边纸、毛太纸
Bamboo paper with rough edges called *Mao Bian* or *Mao Tai*.

起文字的雕版，然后涂以墨汁，以白纸铺在雕版上，经过擦刷后取下晾平，即成一页。这就是原始的印刷术，印刷用纸多选用纸面光滑、纸质均匀、吸墨适量的竹制毛边纸和毛太纸。

Paper and Printing

Printing was an epoch-making invention in the history of civilization, coming only after the writing brush, ink and paper had appeared. The most important condition to the printing birth was paper, whose role was never overestimated.

Before printing began, a copy was made on paper first, then, after proof reading, transferred by carving onto plates as embossment. After ink was applied on the plate, blank paper was spread onto the place to receive repeated brushing until it picked up the characters. Then, it was sent for drying and this was the primitive form of printing. The paper used was often made from bamboo with rough edges but glossy with fine texture and right degree of ink absorption.

- 写样
Writing

- 校对
Proof reading

- 刻版
Engraving

- 刷印
Brush-printing

- 上板
Installing plates

明清时期的纸

明清时期，造纸工艺进一步发展，造纸原料及生产技术都有了很大的突破，出现了许多精品，特别是一些精美的纸笺不仅仅是书画用纸，其本身就是一件赏心悦目的艺术品。如羊脑笺、贡笺、砑花纸、五色粉蜡笺等。

羊脑笺是明代的一种名贵纸，这种纸以存放较久的羊脑和顶烟墨涂于纸上，再经砑光工序制成。其特点是黑如漆，明如镜，用泥金写经，可防虫蛀，历久不坏。

Paper Made During the Ming and Qing Dynasties

During the Ming Dynasty (1368-1644) and the Qing Dynasty (1644-1911) progress was made in both material and making technology. Famous varieties appeared. Some of them, no longer made for painting and calligraphy, were works of art. These varieties included *Yang Nao*, *Gong Jian*, *Ya Hua* and Five-color Pink Wax.

Yang Nao was a very famous and expensive kind made during the Ming Dynasty, made by calendaring with lamb brain and top-class soot ink applied to surface. It is exceptionally black and glossy, perfect for sutra writing in gold characters and able to withstand damage

• 羊脑笺《高上玉皇本行集经三卷》（明）
Three volumes of sutra on *Yang Nao* paper (Ming Dynasty, 1368-1644)

贡笺是明代名纸，制于明宣德年间，是一种加工纸，其制作技艺十分精湛。这种纸有许多品种，如本色纸、五色粉笺、金花五色笺、五色大帘纸、磁青纸等，其颜色是经专门的染料浸染而来的。

研花纸是明清以来一种新的加工纸。纸料为上等较坚韧的皮纸，有厚有薄，图案多为山水、花鸟、鱼虫、龙凤、云纹或水纹，也有人物故事或文字。纸的表面施粉，非常精细，很适于笔墨书写。

- 竹纹研花纸 书札（明）
Letter on *Ya Hua* paper with bamboo lines
(Ming Dynasty, 1368-1644)

五色粉蜡笺也是一种加工纸，始于唐代、盛行于清代。这种纸为多层黏合纸，底料的皮纸施以粉并

from inspects.

Gong Jian was a famous processed variety first appearing during the Xuan De Period of the Ming Dynasty. It had varieties, the original color, five color, golden, five-color big and *Ci Qing*. Their colors came by soaking in special pigments.

Ya Hua paper, as a new variety, was born during the Ming and the Qing Dynasties, made from tough paper in different thickness. It often had patterns like landscape, flower and bird, fish and insects, dragon and phoenix, cloud and water waves, human figures, even written characters. Very fine powder was applied onto surface, very good for writing with brushes.

Wu Se or "five color pink wax paper" came from the Tang Dynasty but reached its peak during the Qing Dynasty. This paper had multiple layers on a tough paper foundation, often dyed into blue, white, pink, pale green or yellow. After being waxed and calendared by hand, it was done. This paper featured waterproof and mothproof, glossy surface and transparency, able to last for a long time.

A passion for making imitations of ancient varieties happened during the Ming and the Qing Dynasties. The Ming

• 蜡笺《御制千尺雪得句》（清）

Wang Youdun's writing after snow, bearing Emperor Qianlong's seal stamp for book collection, on wax paper(Qing Dynasty, 1644-1911)

加染蓝、白、粉红、淡绿、黄等五色，加蜡以手工捶轧砑光制成，故称"五色粉蜡笺"。这种纸的特点是防水性强，表面光滑，透明度好，防虫蛀，可以长久存放。

明清时期还兴起了仿制纸的热潮。明代仿制了唐代的"薛涛笺"和宋代的"金粟山经笺"。这种仿制纸在制作时加入了云母粉，纸面显出光亮耀眼的颗粒，是明代人的创新。清代时仿制的纸品种更多，尤其是康熙、乾隆年间的仿制纸品最为精细，不仅保留了原纸的特点，还用泥金绘制各种精美图案作为装饰，并且清楚标注仿制的时间和品名，供内府收藏和保管。

Dynasty had imitations of Xue Tao paper from the Tang Dynasty and the *Jin Su* sutra paper from the Song Dynasty. With mica powder added to their pulp these imitations shimmered against light. This was a Ming invention. Imitations made during the Qing Dynasty became even more, particularly during the Kang Xi and Qian Long reigns. Not only preserving original features, the imitations had something new to it, say, a decoration painted in gold. They also bore the name of the variety they were after and the time they were made. Usually, they were collected by the interior office of the Forbidden City.

纸的制作流程
Steps of paper making

纸的制作要经过以下步骤：

Paper making had the following steps:

取坯：造纸的第一道工序，是将藤、竹、麻、树皮等原料搜集起来，然后将选好的原料结成捆进行蒸煮、脱皮，最后再将这些毛料浸泡在石灰水里，若干天后取出洗净，这就是制纸的坯料。

Material collection: This was the first step, which meant to select cane, bamboo, hemp and tree bark, and bundle them for steaming, boiling, debarking before they were placed in lime water for a couple days. Then, they were washed clean. By now, the materials were ready.

制料：造纸的重要一步，对皮坯进行反复的浸渍、蒸煮、洗涤和暴晒，其目的是去除杂质，提纯纤维。

Materials processing: A crucial step, which meant repeated soaking, steaming, boiling, washing and drying in the sun. This step was to remove impurities for clean fibers.

③

④

打浆：将经过制料的坯料浸在草木灰水中，历时十多天后即可发酵为浆料。然后把浆料放入臼中，舂成纸浆。

Pulp making: Leave the processed materials in lime water for a dozen of days before they were fermented and pounded into pulp in a mortar.

抄纸（捞纸）：把纸浆倒进石槽里，加胶或者纸药水以及木槿汁，使之具有黏性，然后持竹帘进入水槽，将纸浆抄进帘内以滤去水分并形成纸胎，再将纸胎平放在湿纸板上。

Chao zhi or paper lifting: Pulp in mortar received glue, medicine and hibiscus juice to make it sticky. Then, lowering a bamboo sieve into the pulp and lifting it with a layer of pulp on it. After water was drained away the layer became the rough form of paper to be placed on a wet board.

⑤ 焙纸：等平放在湿纸板上的纸胎叠够一定的张数后，将其压干，然后再把纸一张张揭开，贴到光洁的砖砌的夹墙上。夹墙里烧着柴火，用炙热的墙面把纸烘干。这样，一张手工纸就初步制成了。

Baking: When layers reached the right number they were pressed to release water. Then peel them off sheet by sheet, paste them on a wall with fire inside. The heat will completely dry the paper. By now, a sheep of hand-made paper was done.

加工纸则是在以上步骤完成之后再进行加工制作而成，常见的加工方法有几下几种：

Additional processing was given for paper of special needs. Common additional processing was the following:

砑光：用光滑的卵石在纸面上来回压磨，使纸面光滑。这项工艺在东汉末年就已出现。

Rub very smooth pebbles on paper until the paper became very smooth. This processing first appeared in the late Eastern Han Dynasty.

染色：用有机染料给纸染色，最初染黄色者居多，后来各种色彩的纸纷纷涌现。

Dye with organic pigments into yellow at beginning, more colors later.

施粉：在纸有孔隙的地方用粉加以填补。最初的目的是填补孔隙，后来将它与彩色一起混合，用来调和色彩，色彩斑斓的粉纸由此产生。

Powder application: The original purpose was to fill up tiny holes on paper texture. Later, pigments were added to powder for a colorful look.

• 施过粉的小笺（清）
Paper after receiving powder (Qing Dynasty, 1644-1911)

洒金：洒金的目的是为了使纸面看上去更加绚丽夺目，富丽华贵，通常是在彩色的粉纸上撒上金银粉末。在洒金之前，要在纸面上涂上黏合剂，撒上金银粉末后再进行砑光。

Scattering gold powder: This was to give the paper a very luxurious look by gold or silver powder. The paper received a coat of adhesive first and calendaring after powder was applied.

• 洒金云龙纹色绢纸（清）
Color paper having received gold powder, printed with a cloud and dragon pattern (Qing Dynasty, 1644-1911)

印花：印花有两种方法，一种是印明花，直接将图案印在纸面上；一种是印暗花，是在抄纸过程中将纸压在两块一正一反刻有凸凹花纹图案的木刻版中间，逐幅印制。

Stamping: There were two ways: one was to print a pattern on paper and the other was to squeeze by two patterned wood plates, one in intaglio, the other in relief.

> 纸的种类

　　纸的种类主要是根据不同的造纸原料来划分的，古代用于造纸的原料主要有麻、树皮、藤、竹、草等，因此纸可分为麻纸、皮纸、藤纸、竹纸、草纸等。

　　麻纸是以麻为主要原料制成的纸。从造纸术诞生到东晋时期，麻纸一直是主流用纸。蔡伦造纸所用的原料是破渔网、破布等麻类纤维，所造之纸也属于麻纸。

> Varieties of paper

By materials paper can be classified into different types. Because ancient times used hemp, cane, tree bark, bamboo and weed, paper made from them picked up similar names, hemp paper, bast paper, cane paper, bamboo paper and weed paper.

Hemp paper took hemp as its material. Ever since the birth of paper making to the East Jin dynasty hemp was its major material. The old fishing nets and bits of cloth belonged to this hemp type. So the paper made from them was called hemp paper.

• 麻
Hemp

皮纸是以各种树皮制成的纸，包括桑树皮、楮树皮、青檀树皮、木芙蓉树皮等。皮纸纤维长，纸质洁白细嫩，柔韧性好，张力强，吸水性和透气性好，光滑度高，有清香味，不易变色，保存年代久，是古人书写重要契约及佛教道教经文的首选纸。

● 树皮
Tree bark

藤纸是以藤皮所制的纸，最出名的藤纸是剡藤纸，因产于剡县(今浙江省嵊州市)而得名。其特点是薄、轻、韧、细、白，莹润光泽，坚滑而不凝笔，质地优良。

竹纸主要以嫩竹制成，发明于唐代，宋代以后便普遍推广开来，其产地在江浙一带。竹纸成本低廉，书写流畅，纸面光洁，吸湿性强，纸张整洁、干燥，质薄无碎屑，色泽均匀，无异味。

Bast paper took barks from mulberry, wingceltis and hibiscus as material. Bast paper had long fiber, very white and smooth in appearance and supple. It was highly expansive, hydrophilic, breathy, smooth and fragrant. Bast paper could be kept for a long time without losing its color. Bast paper was often used for copying Buddhist or Taoist sutras and important documents.

Cane paper, as its name suggests, came from the skin of cane. The most famous in this variety came from Shanxian (today's Shengzhou of Zhejiang). Cane paper made there was thin, light, tough, fine, white and glossy, easy for brush tip to move upon.

Bamboo paper was made from

● 藤
Cane

• 竹
Bamboo

草纸是以植物茎类制造的纸，其缺点是比较粗糙，易出墨晕，不适宜书写。

tender bamboo, an invention made during the Tang Dynasty, becoming popular from the Song Dynasty. The biggest production place of this variety was Jiangsu and Zhejiang. Low cost, easy to be written upon, smooth at surface, hydroscopic, neat at format, dry, thin and less breakable, evenly colored and having no funny odor, these were the characteristics of this kind.

Weed paper came from plant stems. This variety had disadvantages: rough in texture, easy for ink to ooze and not very good for writing.

纸的装订

在中国古代，纸的装订形式经历了一个演变的过程。从最初沿袭帛书的卷轴装，再向册页发展，衍生出经折装、旋风装等多种形式。五代时出现了蝴蝶装，后来又改用包背装，最后是线装。

Paper Binding

Paper binding experienced a long progress, from rolls like books on silk at beginning to later albumed paintings, it had many forms before it reached thread binding. One form of this variety named "the butterfly" appeared during the Five-dynasty Period, followed by Bao Bei and finally the thread binding.

• 卷轴装

最早的装订方式，阅读时可逐渐展开，阅毕卷起即可。这种装帧形式至今仍用于书画的装裱。

Roll binding

Roll binding was the earliest form with the advantage of easy unrolling for reading and rolling after reading was done. This form is still used for the mounting of paintings or calligraphic works.

- ## 经折装

将一幅长卷沿着文字版面的间隔中缝，一反一正地折叠起来，形成长方形的一叠，阅读起来比卷轴装方便许多。

Sutra binding

This was to fold a long sheet of paper along the central line straight and reverse alternatively to make a rectangular book. This form was easier to read than the roll binding.

- ## 旋风装

在经折装的基础上，将一张纸对折后一半粘在第一页，一半粘在最后一页，避免散页的问题。

Xuan Feng binding

This was, after sutra binding, folding the paper to reduce its size by half, paste one side of the folded to page one and the other side to the last page. This binding had no loose page problem.

- ## 龙鳞装

又称"鱼鳞装"，是将散页依次序像鱼鳞一样粘在一张卷轴式的纸上。

Long Lin binding

Also named Yu Lin binding this binding was to paste loose pages onto a paper roll like fish scales.

- 蝴蝶装

起源于唐代，流行于宋代的装订形式，由于版面犹如蝴蝶展翅而得名。将有文字的两页对折，将折叠处粘连在硬纸上，翻阅时会出现无字的背面。

Butterfly binding

First seen during the Tang Dynasty but popular during the Song Dynasty, this variety got its name form its resemblance of butterfly. This was to fold two pages with printed sides into folio and paste it onto board paper. When being leafed, unprinted side was shown.

- 包背装

书页背对背地折叠起来，将书页的两边粘在书脊上。避免了蝴蝶装阅读时出现白页的问题。

Bao Bei binding

Each page was folded back to back before being pasted onto the book spine. This binding had no blank page problem as seen in the butterfly binding.

- 线装

用两张半页纸，分置于书页的前后，与书册一起装订，避免了包背装书背处容易破损的问题。

Thread binding

Have two sheets of soft paper bound together with the book, one at the beginning of the book and the other on its end to make the spine stronger.

具有收藏价值的古籍

Collectable Ancient Books

古籍是古纸做成的，很多古纸都是以古籍的形式流传保留至今的。具有收藏价值的古籍有以下几种：

Ancient books had ancient paper in them and much ancient paper that came down in history is seen in this form. The most collectable ancient books are the following:

符合"三性九类"的古籍

"三性"是指具有三种特性的古籍：因古籍年代久远而具有的"历史文物性"；因古籍内容有重要参考价值而具有的"学术资料性"；因古籍的雕版印制考究、插图精美等而具有的"艺术代表性"。

"九类"是指九种古籍：一是元代或元代以前刻印或抄写的书本；二是明代刻印或抄写的书本（版本模糊、流传较多的除外）；三是清代乾隆及乾隆以前流传较少的刻本、抄本；四是太平天国及历代农民革命政权所印行的书本；五是辛亥革命前，在学术研究上有独到见解或有学派特点，以及流传很少的刻本、抄本；六是辛亥革命前反映某一时期、某一领域或某一事件资料方面的稿本，以及较少见的刻本、抄本；七是辛亥革命前有名人、学者批校、题跋，或抄录前人批校而有参考价值的刻本、抄本；八是在印刷上能反映中国印刷技术发展、代表一定时期印刷水平的各种活字本、套印本，或有较精版画的刻本；九是明代印谱、清代集古印谱、名家篆刻的钤印本、有特色或有亲笔题记的书本。

Ancient Books of Three Unique Significance in Nine Categories:

Three unique significances mean "historical significances" ,because of being printed centuries ago; "academic significance" ,because of the information they give; "artistic significance" from exquisite engraving and illustrations.

The nine categories are as follows: Printed or hand-written in or before the Yuan Dynasty(1279-1368); printed or hand-written in the Ming Dynasty(1368-1644) or prior to the Ming Dynasty (not including less clear editions or the edition with many copies in circulation); printed or hand-written with few copies in circulation during and before the Qian Long Reign of the Qing Dynasty (1736-1795); books issued by farmers regimes like the "Taiping Heavenly Kingdom" (1851-1864); academically valuable books of rare editions; books and records about a certain period of time, a certain event in history or a field either printed or hand-written prior to the 1911 Revolution; printed or hand-written editions with inscriptions from or annotated by famous personage; books that may show the progress of Chinese printing technology, printed with movable types or chromatograph edition or with highly artistic illustrations; collections of stamp prints or inscriptions or carvings from famous personage of the Ming and the Qing Dynasties.

- 试卷（明）
  Test paper (Ming Dynasty, 1368-1644)

- 王国维手校线装本
  《冷斋夜话》（清）
  Leng Zhai Ye Hua or Idle Talks in Cold Study at Night, a thread bound edition annotated by Wang Guowei (Qing Dynasty, 1644-1911)

特殊版本的古籍

　　古籍的版本是决定其收藏价值的重要因素。通常，木刻本价值高于石印本，石印本价值高于铅印本。此外，初版的古籍价值要高于再版和重复印刷的。

Special Ancient Editions

Edition determines the value of a book collected. Usually, block printed edition is more valuable than lithography edition and a lithography edition is more valuable than a stereotype edition. First edition and the first print are more valuable than later editions and later prints.

纸张轻盈的古籍

纸张的轻盈程度也是决定古籍价值高低的一个因素，古籍纸张越轻，用纸越高档，收藏价值越高。

Ancient Books Printed on Paper of Light Weight

Weight of paper also determines the value of an ancient book. The lighter the paper, which means better quality, the more valuable the book is.

● 麻纸　浙刻本南岳旧稿1、2（宋）

Old manuscripts on hemp paper, volume I and volume II (Song Dynasty, 960-1279)

题材独特的古籍

题材内容越独特的古籍具有越高的收藏价值。一般来说，在经史子集里，子集类古籍的收藏价值相对较高。明清以后的古籍，则以那些记载了重大历史事件的工具书，传记书，记录特殊年代、特殊事件的古籍最有收藏价值。

Ancient Books with Unique Subject Matter

The more unique the subject matter the more valuable the book is. Among all the books of classical studies philosophy and literature books have a bigger value, so are the books after the Ming and the Qing Dynasties of a significant event, biography or chronicles.

发行量少的古籍

"物以稀为贵"是收藏的一大准则。很多古籍之所以价格高昂，就是因为各种原因导致能较完整流传下来的很少。

Editions with Little Print Run

When a thing becomes rare, it is precious—this is a common saying among collectors. The high value of ancient books is determined by their small numbers of complete ones that have come down to present day.

古纸的保存

古纸的保存要注意防潮、防虫、防晒、防干裂、防烟熏和油污、防折叠等。

防潮：久藏的古纸一旦受潮，就会出现水渍和霉点。防止古纸受潮的办法是在纸的外面用一层皮纸包裹，然后放于盒中，置于干燥、凉爽、通风之处。

防虫：虫会咬噬古纸，造成古纸破损，可在存纸的地方放置一些驱避剂，如麝香、云草等。

防晒：古纸经过强烈的阳光照射后很容易裂开，纸色也会变黄，所以应尽量避免阳光、灯光的直射。

防烟熏和油污：古纸不应长期放在有烟气熏染的地方，在检视古纸时切忌手上有油污。另外，尽量不要用手直接抚摸纸。

防折叠：古纸应尽量用卷的方式来收藏，折叠容易破坏其品相。

● 玉霜戏曲抄本
Hand-copied script, bearing an ancient play script

Keeping of Ancient Paper

The keeping of ancient paper must be damp free, mothproof, out of sunshine, away from smoke, oil and folding threats and seasoning crack free.

Moisture proof: Affected with damp mildew and water marks appear. Prevention against this is to wrap ancient paper with a sheet of bast paper before leaving it in a box, to be placed in a dry, shady and ventilated place.

Mothproof: Inspects make a big threat to the keeping and insect repellents like musk or cloud weed left next to the paper work.

Out of sunshine: Direct sunshine makes ancient paper crack and turn yellow so ancient paper should never be left in sunshine or exposed to lamplight.

Keep the paper off oil and smoke. Ancient paper should be kept off either smoke or oil, even the oil on hand. Direct contacts should be avoided.

Ancient paper should be rolled for keeping. Folding seriously damages its looks.

● 宣统御制宣纸（清）

The *Xuan* paper made during the Xuan Tong Reign for royal use only (Qing Dynasty, 1644-1911)

砚

Ink slab

　　砚，是研墨的工具，同笔、墨、纸一起共同记录着中国古老的历史和悠久的文化。砚的材质和式样丰富多彩，是文房四宝中流传至今数量最多的。砚的制作融合了中国传统雕刻、绘画、文学等因素，凝结了众多制砚匠人的智慧。

Like the writing brush, ink sticks and paper, the ink slab in different fashions and materials has recorded Chinese history and culture. Of the four treasures of the study, ancient ink slabs that have survived history are more than the rest three. Their making shows the values of traditional Chinese sculpture, painting and literature. It was a product of collective wisdom from craftsmen.

> 砚的历史

砚的历史十分悠久,最初与研磨棒一起配套使用。砚的材质很多,但除了石砚、瓷砚、玉砚几种,其他材质的古砚目前已很少见到完整之物。

砚的发端

砚,在汉代以前叫"研",从字面意思来看,是研墨的工具。砚出现得非常早,从考古资料来看,最迟在新石器时代仰韶文化时期(距今7000～5000年)就已经出现人造砚。1980年,在陕西省临潼县一座仰韶文化初期墓葬中就出土了一套研墨工具。

汉代以前的砚,都配有一支研石棒,是用来研墨的。那时的墨是墨丸,不能单独用手握住,需要用

> History of Ink Slab

Ink slabs have a long history. At beginning, they were used together with a grounding stick. Ink slabs are in many varieties and different materials yet apart from stone, porcelain and jade, ink slabs of other kinds, compete ones in particular, are seldom seen today.

The beginning

As suggested by its name in Chinese, ink slabs are a tool to make ink. Their appearance came fairly early, in the Yangshao Cultural Period of the Neolithic Age (about 7000~5000 years ago) at the latest. In 1980, a set of tools for making ink was discovered in a tomb in Lintong of Shaanxi from the early Yangshao Culture.

Before the Han Dynasty ink slabs had a stick to go with for grinding ink

研棒压住才能进行研磨。1975 年，湖北云梦睡虎地秦墓出土了一方用鹅卵石加工制成的砚，砚形为圆饼形，其上无纹饰，配有研棒一支。同时出土的还有墨和笔，这是中国迄今发现的最早的书写砚。

- 颜料研磨器（仰韶文化）
  这件研磨器带有盖，配有一支石质研磨棒，旁边有黑色的颜料，被视为中国砚的"鼻祖"。
  Pigment grinder (Yangshao Culture, about 7000~5000 years ago)
  This grinder has a lid and a stick with black pigments nearby. It is viewed as the ancestor of the ink stone.

汉代（前206—公元220）时，砚的材质以石、陶为主，砚的使用已十分普遍，但大部分都配有研棒。直到东汉末年，墨的形制从墨丸改为可以手执的块墨，研棒才逐渐消失。这一时期，砚的形制也富于变化，常见的有圆形的石砚、龟形的陶砚等。

balls, not sticks. The ball easily slipped away on the stone so keeping it in place by a stick was necessary. In 1975, an ink slab made from a pebble was unearthed from a Qin tomb in Yunmeng of Hubei Province. It was round in shape, unornamented but had a grinding stick. Together with it were an ink stick and a writing brush. This set makes the oldest ink slab ever discovered in China.

- 石砚（秦）
  Ink slab, stone (Qin Dynasty, 211 B.C.-206 B.C.)

Ink slabs of stone and pottery were popular during the Han Dynasty (206 B.C.-220 A.D.) and they still went with a grinding stick. Grinding sticks existed until the late Eastern Han Dynasty when ink changed from balls to sticks that hands could hold them easily. The shape of ink slab became diversified, the most common being round like a stone or pottery turtle.

- 石砚（汉）
  Ink slab, stone (Han Dynasty, 206
  B.C.-220 A.D.)

- 盘龙石砚（汉）
  Ink slab, stone, ornamented with dragon
  (Han Dynasty, 206 B.C.-220 A.D.)

魏晋南北朝时期的砚

魏晋南北朝时期，墨的形制不断改进，研磨棒因此彻底消失。砚的材质仍以陶、石为主。陶砚在南方盛行，多为圆形、箕形、长方形，并且都有蹄形砚足，使砚的高

Ink Slabs Made During the Wei, Jin, Southern and Northern Periods

Due to incessant improvements made during the Wei, the Jin and the Southern and Northern Dynasties (220-589) ink slabs no longer needed grinding sticks, though their materials were still stone or

- 《北齐校书图》【局部】杨子华（北齐）
  魏晋南北朝及隋唐时期的砚台有不少是仿辟雍（西周天子所设大学，其园如璧，四面环水）之形设计。砚台四周留有深槽储水，中心隆起，以众多的柱足承托砚身。
  Proof reading (detail) by Yang Zihua (Northern Qi Dynasty, 550-577)
  Many slabs were fashioned after the construction of West Zhou's royal academy, which was enclosed by a circular wall and having water around. Ink slabs, similarly, had a ditch to keep water, central part higher and feet at the bottom to support the slab.

度增加。砚足的出现是为了适应当时席地坐和用矮几书写的要求。砚足还有三足、四足、五足、六足、八足之分。在中国北方地区则流行石砚，多为长方形和四方形，常在上面雕刻人物、花鸟等精美图案。

　　另外，魏晋南北朝时期的制砚工艺精进，金属砚、瓷砚、金砚、银砚等相继出现，这些材质名贵的砚大都做工十分精美。1957年，安徽省肥东县草庙乡大孤堆出土了一件南朝铜鎏金蟾蜍砚，砚上镶嵌着红、黄、蓝等各色宝石，此砚反映了魏晋南北朝时期制砚工艺的高超。

隋唐时期的砚

　　隋唐时期，由于书画纸的出现、毛笔与墨的精进，书画艺术取得卓越成就，砚的使用也更加广泛。

　　这一时期一种陶制的"澄泥砚"大受欢迎，因其具有"含津益墨"的性能而著名。同时人们发现天然砚石的品质要好于人造的材质，在广东、安徽、甘肃、山东等地，都发现了大量制砚的名贵石料，产生了端砚、歙砚等名砚。除

pottery. Pottery ones were more seen in China's south, mostly round, rectangular or in a dustpan shape having feet to increase height. The feet were needed when writing while sitting on floor or on a very low stool. The number of feet varied, from three to four, five, six and even eight. In China's north stone ink stones were popular, most being rectangular or square ornamented with carved human figures, birds or flowers.

By then, workmanship was much improved, with new varieties available like metal, porcelain, gold or silver. Most of the slabs were elaborately made. In 1957, in Feidong of Anhui Province, a bronze gilt ink slab from the Southern Dynasty (420-589) was brought to light, on which were inlaid precious stones in different colors. This ink slab showed the superb craftsmanship of the time.

Ink Slabs Made During the Sui and the Tang Dynasties

Due to the invention of writing and painting paper, the progress made in writing brushes and ink sticks and also because of a higher level painting and calligraphy art reached, ink slabs

了石材之外，还有其他特色材质的砚，如瓦当砚，其选材于秦汉魏晋时期废毁的宫殿残砖、剩瓦，其中不少来自于名传千古的阿房宫、未央宫。晚唐五代时期，在北方还流行一种铁砚，砚身有柄，可执可握，发墨性能佳。

• 白釉辟雍砚（隋）
White glazed ink slab (Sui Dynasty, 581-618)

• 鸟纽辟雍盖砚（唐）
Ink slab with feet and a bird-knob lid (Tang Dynasty, 618-907)

during the Sui (581-618) and the Tang Dynasties(618-907) gained a popularity it had never had before.

Pottery ink slabs made from *Cheng Ni* clay became popular because of its unusual ink-friendly property. People realized natural materials were better than man-made materials. In Guangdong, Anhui, Gansu and Shandong, nice materials for ink slabs were found. Famous varieties like those made in Duanzhou and Shexian became known. Apart from stone, tile ends from ruined palaces of the Qin (221 B.C.-206 B.C.), the Han (206 B.C.-220 A.D.), the Wei (220-280) and the Jin (265-420) Periods became a much favored material. Some of them came from famous E Pang or Wei Yang. In the late Tang Dynasty (618-901) or the Five-dynasty (907-960) Periods that followed, in China's north, iron ink slabs with a handle, convenient for holding and very ink-friendly, became a fashion.

Most of the ink slabs during the Sui and the Tang Dynasties were either round or in the shape of a dustpan. Most of them had no obvious hallow to keep ink, simply having a side higher than the other for tidying brush tips. In

隋唐时期，砚的造型以圆形和箕形为主，砚上没有砚堂和砚池，一侧砚足略高，使砚面略有斜倾，方便捺笔。箕形因与"凤"和"凤"字形状相似，又称"凤（凤）字砚"或"凤凰池"。唐末五代后，高型家具渐渐兴起，于是无足平台式的砚台开始流行，砚的形制也逐渐丰富起来。

Chinese, the character "dustpan" was quite like the character "phoenix" in resemblance. So ink slabs in the shape of dustpan was also called "phoenix ink slab". After the Tang Dynasty and the Five-dynasty Periods, taller furniture appeared. So flat ink stones without feet became popular. Their shapes became more diversified.

砚池：又名"砚海"，指砚的低洼处，用来存积清水或墨汁。
Yan Chi: the lower spot to keep water or ink.

砚岗：砚堂中间稍高的部分，四周成斜坡，使墨汁可以流向砚池。
Yan Gang: the ridge with a slope on all sides to make ink flow easily to *Yan Chi*.

砚侧：砚的侧面，也可用作镌刻铭记之位。
Yan Ce: the side of the slab, a possible place to receive inscriptions.

砚边：砚堂周围略高的边缘带。
Yan Bian: the edge of *Yan Tang*, usually higher.

砚额：又名"砚头"，指砚的上部较其他三边更宽的部位，一般主要纹饰都安排在砚额。
Yan E: also called the head, referring to the thicker side of the slab, often being the place to receive ornamentation.

砚背：砚的背面，又叫"砚底"，可用来镌刻铭记诗词。
Yan Bei: the back or the bottom of the slab, likely to be inscribed with a poem.

砚堂：又名"墨堂"，为研墨之处。
Yan Tang: the spot to grind ink.

● 石砚（唐）
Ink slab, stone (Tang Dynasty, 618-907)

石砚的制作
The Making of a Stone Ink Slab

一方砚从砚石开采出来到制成成品，要经过选料、打磨、雕刻、配盒四个步骤。

From raw material to a completed ink slab there were many steps: material selection, carving, polishing and casing.

- 切割好的石坯
  The cut stone

- 四边整平的石坯
  The stone that has been polished on sides

- 人工铲平的石坯（砚璞）
  The stone that has been polished flat and smooth, now called *Yan Pu*.

选料：采出的砚石需要经过筛选，将瑕疵、裂痕、白皮、底板、顶板等部分剔除，保留"石肉"，然后对石料分等列级。根据石料的花纹进行巧妙的设计，做到"因石构图"，突出砚石的特色亮点，经过这一步加工的石坯称为"砚璞"。

Material selection: The stone material selected had to be scrutinized carefully to get rid of even the tiniest flaw. Only the best part in the middle was kept. Then, it was rated to different classes before a decorative pattern was designed to match the material's veins. Every stone was different and each had something unusual to be highlighted. By now, the stone was called Yan Pu, meaning "a selected stone to be worked on".

- 打磨
  Polishing

- 雕刻
  Carving

打磨：以油石和河沙磨砚璞，以去其凿口和刀路，然后用滑石打磨的工序。通过这一步可使砚石变得细腻、光滑。在经过"浸墨润石"、褪墨等工序处理后便能制成精良的砚石。

Polishing: This refers to the process of using very smooth stone and sand to polish, to get rid of any mark left from chiseling or cutting. Talc was used for smoothing. After this the stone was to receive the last two steps: receiving and removing ink for the first time.

雕刻：是对砚璞进行艺术处理与加工的工序。先要对砚石进行设计、创作，再运用深刀（高浮雕）、浅刀（低浮雕）、细刻、线刻等方法进行雕刻。

Carving: Carving was to ornament the ink slab. The design made was transferred onto the stone by cutting knives in high or low relief. Line carving or detail carving was common.

配盒：精美的砚都要配上匣盒，以起到防尘和保护砚石的作用。砚盒一般都是木制的，而且多选用名贵木材。砚盒的造型依照砚石的形状而定。

Casing: A fine ink slab must be cased to keep from dust. Usually a case was wood of an expensive kind in the shape that matched the slab.

- 雕刻好的砚台
  The carved ink slab

宋元时期的砚

自宋代开始，砚就以石砚为主导，开发出了更多可用于制砚的新石料，如淄州金雀石、高唐州紫石、宿州乐石、登州石、戎州石、泸州石、蔡州白石等。石砚受到重视，一方面是因为它的发墨效果好，符合书画艺术家对研墨的高要求，另一方面是文人对砚石本身的色彩、纹理也产生了浓厚的兴趣。韩琦、蔡襄、王安石、苏轼、苏

Ink Slabs Made During the Song and the Yuan Dynasties

From the Song Dynasty(960-1279), the chief material for ink slabs was stone. Apart from old types of stone, new ones like *Jin Que* from Zizhou, *Zi Shi* from Gaotang, *Le Shi* from Suzhou and the stones from Dengzhou, Rongzhou, Luzhou and Caizhou were valued. One reason for their popularity was their ink-friendliness that met artists' need for ink grinding; another reason was the

辙、黄庭坚等宋代文豪都写过不少赞美石砚色彩、花纹的诗篇。

- 抄手石砚（宋）
  Stone ink slab (Song Dynasty, 960-1279)

宋代时，石砚的造型也更加多样化。如歙砚就有月、圭、莲叶、古钱、蟾蜍、琴、辟雍、凤字等四十余种造型。当时文人还热衷于为石砚制作铭文，镌刻在砚的侧面或砚底、砚盖、砚屏上，由此开了后世

- 蝉形歙砚（宋）
  Cicada-shaped ink slab, Shexian style
  (Song Dynasty, 960-1279)

favorable remarks from literary giants like Han Qi, Cai Xiang, Wang Anshi, Su Shi… on these stones' unique color and veins. The poems they wrote excited the public.

- 玉带砚（宋）
  Jade ribbon ink slab (Song Dynasty, 960-1279)

More shapes appeared during the Song Dynasty (960-1279), and in the *She* school some slabs were fashioned after plants, animals, musical instruments, royal academy of the Western Zhou Dynasty (1046 B.C.-771 B.C.), written characters… Scholars had a strong interest in inscribing the stone. Carvings might appear on the sides, bottom, lid and body of a slab. Later generations followed, as was seen during the Yuan Dynasty (1279-1368), a very bold but simple style characteristic of the Mongolian personality was seen in many designs. It was during about this time that a unique kind called *Nuan Yan*, or

书写砚铭的先河。元代则将粗犷的民族特色注入砚的造型中，体现出朴拙的时代风格。此时还出现了暖砚，制砚时工匠在砚台下部留出空间，可置火加热，防止墨液冻结。

宋代还出现了有关砚的专著，如苏易简的《文房四谱》中的《砚谱》、米芾的《砚史》、唐积的《歙州砚谱》等。

"heatable ink slab" appeared. This type had a place reserved on its lower part to receive heating from fire, to keep ink from freezing.

Writings about ink slabs appeared during the Song Dynasty like the Ink Slab Chapter in *Wen Fang Si Pu*, or *The Four Treasures of the Study* by Su Yijian, *History of Ink Slabs* by Mi Fu and *Varieties of Ink Slabs from Shezhou* by Tang Ji.

● 陶箕形砚（元）
Pottery dustpan-like ink slab (Yuan Dynasty, 1279-1368)

欧阳修与歙、端二砚

欧阳修（1007—1073），庐陵（今江西吉安）人，宋代著名文学家、史学家，他是爱砚之人。

欧阳修平时用的砚台是端砚，自从结识茶馆老板欧阳徽后，改用歙砚。欧阳徽送给欧阳修一方双龙戏珠金星砚。此砚星光闪闪，手感柔嫩润滑，欧阳修爱不释手，赞其为"宝砚"，并将端砚和歙砚作了一番比较，认为歙砚远胜于端砚。

Ouyang Xiu with *She* and *Duan* Style Ink Slabs

Ouyang Xiu (1007-1073), a native from Luling (present-day Ji'an of Jiangxi Province), a famous Song writer and historian, also a famed ink slab lover.

After he came to know the teahouse owner Ouyang Hui, Ouyang Xiu switched from *Duan* style ink slab to a *She* style one. The teahouse owner gave him an ink slab with shining stars on surface and ornamentation of two dragons playing with a pearl. The slab felt very soft, tender and smooth, not like stone. Ouyang Xiu took it as a treasure. He was convinced the *She* style was much better than the *Duan* style.

米芾索砚

米芾（1051—1107），宋代著名的书画家、鉴赏家、收藏家，性格狂放，人称"米癫"。他能诗文、擅书画，精于鉴赏，爱好收藏。

米芾爱砚至深。一次宋徽宗让米芾到宫中写字，并让他使用御桌上的方砚。米芾写完后，手捧御砚，对皇帝说："此砚我已用过，皇上不能再用，就将砚给我吧。"宋徽宗不觉大笑，将砚赐给了他。米芾随即将砚台装入怀中，不管墨汁四处飞溅，跑回家去。

米芾不仅爱砚、藏砚，还不断地加以研究，著有《砚史》一书，书中对各种砚台的产地、色泽、细润、工艺都作了论述。

Mi Fu Asked For An Ink Slab

Mi Fu, (1051-1107), a Song-dynasty painter, calligrapher, art connoisseur and collector, a man who refused to be bound by conventional ideas. He had a nickname: crazy Mi. Yet his attainments in literary writing, painting, calligraphy, artistic criticism and art collection were amazing.

His love for ink slabs was legendary. Once, he was sent by Emperor Hui Zong to do calligraphy in the place. He was allowed to use the emperor's square ink slab on the desk. After he finished writing he held the slab in hand. "I have used this one," said him, "so it is improper for your majesty to use it again. Why not give it to me?" At this, the emperor laughed and granted his request. Mi Fu instantly pocketed the slab without even cleaning the ink on it and ran back home as fast as his legs could take him.

Not only a lover and a collector, Mi Fu was also a researcher who wrote *The History of Ink Slabs*, in which he detailed different varieties, their home places, unique characteristics and different making technology.

● 米芾像
Mi Fu

明清时期的砚

明清时期，砚的发展达到顶峰，出现了很多精雕细琢的精品砚。明代时，对砚石的质地要求更高。为了得到上乘的砚石，人们重新发掘被水淹没多年的端石老坑，发现了比前代更为优质且细润美丽的石头。文人们赋予这些砚石以美名，如青花、蕉叶白、冰纹、鱼脑冻等。

在这一时期，砚雕艺术人才辈出，雕刻技术和制作工艺都达到历史最高水平，出现众多的砚雕流派。江南的砚雕图纹清秀隽永，做工高雅脱俗，人称"浙派"；广

Ink Slabs Made During the Ming and the Qing Dynasties

Ink slabs making technology peaked during the Ming (1368-1644) and the Qing Dynasties(1644-1911) with many master works appearing. The Ming Dynasty put a much tougher request to the quality. In order to get a quality slab people dug into old mining pits flooded by water for years, where they found stones of even better quality. Scholars named these stones by the veins they had.

This period of history saw master makers with legendary skills. Also, different schools appeared: those made in Jiangnan, described as "Zhejiang School", featured nice workmanship and

• 雕人物端砚（清）
Duan ink slab with carved human figure (Qing Dynasty, 1644-1911)

东、福建的砚雕纹饰丰满，图案繁复，人称"广作"；宫廷用砚材料考究，做工规整，带有一股富贵气，被称为"宫作"。另外，文人用砚以风雅见长，往往透出一种书卷气；民间用砚因注重实用，不太讲究材质与做工，风格质朴。这些不同地区、不同风格的砚雕最终汇成了砚雕艺术的三大流派——粤派、徽派和苏派。晚清民国时期又出现了海派，使得砚雕工艺更加灿烂。

patterns of elegant simplicity; those made in Guangdong and Fujian, described as "Guangdong style", showed impressive decoration in noble and luxurious motif; ink slabs made for royal use struck with luxury were called "palatial style"; slabs for scholars showed a graceful academic pursuit, while the slabs for common people were simple and practical in use, didn't worry much for the material used or the craftsmanship. Together, they made three schools of the time: the Guangdong, Jiangsu and Anhui schools. In the late Qing Dynasty or during the early years of the Republic, a new school appeared in Shanghai to make it four.

• 宜兴雕龙砚（清）
Ink slab with dragon, made in Yixing (Qing Dynasty, 1644-1911)

李时珍采药得歙砚

李时珍（1518—1593），蕲州（今湖北蕲春）人，中国古代伟大的医学家、药物学家。他历时27年完成医学名著《本草纲目》，在中国传统医学上的成就名满天下，可是他巧得歙砚的故事却鲜为人知。

传说一次李时珍到山上采集百草时，见一农妇晕倒在草丛中，她的手背因被蛇咬而肿胀起来。李时珍用药草敷在她的伤口上，不一会儿农妇便醒了过来。农妇谢过李时珍后，请求他为自己染病的公婆治病，李时珍答应下来并随她来到家中。在为她公婆把过脉后，李时珍问道："家中可有笔墨？"农妇将笔、墨、纸和砚拿来。李时珍见其中的砚石质坚细，砚上两条龙栩栩如生，砚池滋润，十分惊叹。农妇见状说："这是我家祖传的'黄龙戏珠砚'，不用倒水，只要在砚台上敲三下，砚池里就有水了。"李时珍用笔在砚台上敲了三下，果然水满砚池。李时珍赞道："奇砚也。"李时珍开过药方后，砚台便干干净净，无一点墨迹，像没有使用过的一样。

李时珍用了七天的时间将农妇公公、婆婆的病都治好了。农妇一家人对他感激不尽，便将"黄龙戏珠砚"送给了李时珍。相传李时珍用这方宝砚完成了《本草纲目》的编写工作。

Bumping Into A Nice Ink Slab

Li Shizhen (1518-1593), a native of Qizhou (today's Qichun of Hubei Province), a famous medical scientist in ancient China who enjoyed a tremendous fame for *The Compendium of Materia Medica*, an epic work out of 27 years of hard working. However, few people know the story he bumped into a *She* ink slab.

On a trip to collect medicinal herbs in mountains, legend says, Li Shizhen saw an unconscious woman in weed, her hand swollen from a snake bite. Li Shizhen quickly applied herbal medicine to the wound. After the woman came to and thanked Li Shizhen, she asked him to see her parents-in-law who had been seriously ill. At her home, and after taking the pulse of the two old people, Li Shizhen asked if they had kept any writing stuff at home. At this the woman hastily brought him paper, an ink slab and a writing brush. Li Shizhen was amazed at the unique slab she had brought, made with very solid stone in the finest texture imaginable and two dragons carved on its top. Its "pool" was well moistened for use. "This is our family heirloom", the woman said. "You needn't fill with water, simply knock the slab gently for three times and the pool will be filled up." Sure enough, after Li Shizhen did what she said the pool did have water to its brim. "Unbelievable," Li Shizhen exclaimed. The moment he finished prescription, the ink slab became very clean as if never used.

It took him 7 days to cure the old couple. Out of gratitude they gave him the ink slab as a gift. With the slab, he finished his epic work *The Compendium of Material Medica*.

明清时期的砚雕流派

Popular Carving Styles During the Ming and the Qing Dynasties

粤派砚雕艺术

粤派以端砚雕为代表，其风格形成于明代，俗称"广作"。雕刻手法以细刻、线刻和浅浮雕为主，适当穿插深刀雕刻，以花鸟、鱼虫、走兽、山水、人物、仿古器皿、龙凤瑞兽、秋叶、棉豆、玉兰等喜庆吉祥题材为主，形象生动，富有变化。

The Guangdong Style

Represented by *Duan* ink slabs, the Guangdong style appearing in the Ming Dynasty(1368-1644) featured highly exquisite line or low relief carvings. This style also had some, though not many, high reliefs for life-like human figures, flowers, birds, animals, antiques, crops and plants, all being auspicious symbols in Chinese belief.

• 龙凤砚（清）

Dragon and phoenix ink slab (Qing Dynasty, 1644-1911)

徽派砚雕艺术

徽派以歙砚雕为代表，雕刻以浮雕浅刻为主，间或出现深刀雕刻，不作立体的镂空雕，手法细腻，层次分明。徽派砚雕构图多方圆规整，砚边多宽厚，常饰以传统纹样和各种变异纹饰，使得整个砚的造型雍容大方，格调简明。

The Anhui Style

Represented by She ink slabs, this style featured low relief carving with very occasional high relief works but never three-dimensional hollow-outs, all conducted by a very exquisite method to show images arranged on different layers. Most of the carvings of this school were made square or round. Their thick sides often had traditional lines as decoration, having a beauty of simple but graceful kind.

• 歙石长方形砚（明）

Rectangular She ink slab (Ming Dynasty, 1368-1644)

苏派砚雕艺术

苏派砚雕追求平淡、雅逸的风格，表现高雅古典之气，讲求刀法的精致，其构图疏朗，意境高远。苏派砚以随形砚为主，追求简朴古雅、自然华美的艺术境界。

The Jiangsu-style Carving

This style featured simple elegance but profound message, exquisite carving technique to convey a noble aspiration. Patterns carved were often to follow the shape of the slab. Elegant simplicity and a refined taste made the key words for this style.

• 碧玉"莲叶"随形砚（清）
Green jade ink slab of lotus leaves
(Qing Dynasty, 1644-1911)

海派砚雕

晚清民国时期，上海地区出现了以写实为主要风格的砚雕流派，史称"海派砚雕"。制砚以仿自然物体为主，如鸟兽、草虫、花果，以及古钟、蘑菇等，精工巧妙，写实性极强。

The Shanghai Style

Shanghai style appearing during the late Qing Dynasty(1644-1911) and the Republican years showed a realistic pursuit. Most of its subjects were natural things in life like birds, animals, grass and insects, flowers and fruits, ancient bells and mushroom, all rendered highly realistic in great detail.

• 端石瓜蝶砚（清）
Duan ink slab (Qing Dynasty, 1644-1911)

> 古砚的种类

按照材质的不同，古砚可以分为石砚、泥陶砚、瓷砚、漆木砚、玉砚、金属砚等几类，其中以石砚为主流。

石砚取材于天然石料，多是江河中常年被雨水冲刷的石头。石砚自汉代起才开始应用，唐代时盛行并广泛运用起来，明清时期达到顶峰。尽管石砚出现的时间与泥陶

> Varieties of Antique Ink Slabs

By materials, ancient ink slabs were stone, pottery, clay, porcelain, lacquered wood, jade and metal, but the majority being stone.

Stone ink slabs came from the stones after being washed by rainwater for years. Earliest stone ink slabs appeared during the Han Dynasty (206 B.C.-220 A.D.), popular during the Tang Dynasty(618-907) and reaching

- 石砚（唐）
  Stone ink slab (Tang Dynasty, 618-907)

- 石砚（明）
  Stone ink slab (Ming Dynasty, 1368-1644)

砚、瓷砚等相比较晚，但石砚的品质居于众砚之首，是最受欢迎，也是收藏最热的砚台品种。

泥陶砚是唐代以前使用最多的砚，由于泥陶砚较易破碎，所以存世者极少，比较著名的有汉代"十二峰陶砚"、唐代的"二十二柱足圆陶砚"，均收藏于故宫博物院。泥陶砚包括陶砚、澄泥砚、瓦砚、砖砚、缸砚、紫砂砚等类型。

● 瓦当砚（汉）
Tile-end ink slab (Han Dynasty, 206 B.C.-220 A.D.)

● 福禄寿澄泥砚（现代）
Cheng-clay ink slab of happiness, officialdom and longevity (contemporary product)

their pinnacle during the the Ming Dynasties(1368-1644) and Qing (1644-1911). Though younger than pottery, clay and porcelain ones stone slabs had every reason to top others as the most popular, collectable and sought after.

The clay-pottery ink slabs were popular before the Tang Dynasty but because of their fragility very few have come down in history. Among the existent were "12-peak ink slab" from the Han Dynasty and "22-feet round ink slab" from the Tang Dynasty, both now in the collection of the Palace Museum. Other kinds in this variety were pottery, clay, tile, brick, vat or *Zi Sha* (boccaro, or simply purple sand).

Porcelain ink slabs first appeared during the Wei and the Jin Periods and were seen in all later dynasties. Apart from the spot to grind ink, it was glazed by fire. During the Ming and the Qing Dynasties, due to matured firing technology some famous porcelain slabs were made, many bearing the year of making and the names of the workshop and the maker, thus highly artistically valuable. Because of hardness and less ink-friendly, they were more for display than for practical use.

瓷砚最早出现于魏晋时期，此后历代皆有制作。瓷砚除砚堂中间的研墨处外全身上釉，然后以高温烧结而成。明清时期，陶瓷烧制技术的发展使得精品瓷砚大量生产，砚上多留有制作时间、作坊名称以及工匠姓名等，极具艺术性。瓷砚因其瓷胎过硬，磨墨时不易下墨，实用性较差，故多作观赏陈设之用。

漆木砚是用木材为胎，再以生漆髹成砚堂而制成的砚。其色似澄泥，可与石砚媲美。漆木砚在清代曾风靡一时。

玉砚是以玉制作的砚。由于玉的硬度高，雕琢比石砚、陶砚困难，所以玉砚大多形制简单。玉砚质地细腻、坚实，但因其不发墨、不吸水，实用性不强，故只作搛笔和收藏之用。

金属砚以金、银、铜、铁、锡等金属制成，以铜砚较为常见。金属砚不常用于书写。

• 褐釉兽座箕形瓷砚（唐）
Glazed brown animal ink slab, porcelain (Tang Dynasty, 618-907)

Lacquered wood ink slabs were in a color close to the *Cheng*-clay, almost as nice as stone ones. This kind of ink slabs was popular during the Qing Dynasty.

Jade ink slabs took jade as the material. But because of the toughness of jade processing, which was more difficult than on other kinds, most jade slabs were in a simple shape. They were hard, fine in texture, absorbing less ink or water, so less practical in use. They were only for collection or tidying brush tips.

Metal ink slabs took gold, silver, bronze, iron or tin as materials but bronze ones were more than others. Seldom was a metal slab used for writing.

• 青玉鹅式砚（清）
Goose ink slab, gray jade (Qing Dynasty, 1644-1911)

砚的基本形制
Basic Forms

砚的形制多种多样，为文房增添了不少情趣。主要形制有几何形砚、动物形砚、植物形砚、箕形砚、抄手砚、圈足砚、随形砚、暖砚等。

Ink slabs in different shapes made a study interesting. Common ones were geometric, animal or plant shapes, dustpan shape, handled or feeted, the shape to follow the shape of the material and slabs that could be heated in cold weather.

几何形砚是指形状为圆形、椭圆形、长方形、方形、八角形等规则形状的砚台，其中方形砚和长方形砚最为常见。

The geometrical meant round, oval, rectangular, square or octagonal shapes. Of all, the square and rectangular were the most common.

- 端石灵芝长方砚（清）

Rectangular *Duan* ink slab with polyporus lucidus
(Qing Dynasty, 1644-1911)

动物形砚是以动物为形制的砚，题材以神兽形象的动物为多，寓意吉祥，也有一些以现实中的动物为题材的，如牛形砚、鹅式砚、鱼形砚等。

Legendary animals were favored images for those fashioned after animals because of the auspicious message they carried. Some took animals in life like ox, goose or fish.

- 澄泥卧牛形砚（明）

Ox ink slab, *Cheng*-clay (Ming Dynasty, 1368-1644)

植物形砚是模仿某些植物形状的砚，常见的有竹节砚、蕉叶砚、荷叶砚、荔枝砚、蘑菇砚等。

Common plants for ink slabs to be fashioned after were bamboo joints, banana or lotus leaves, litchi or mushrooms.

• **白玉荷叶式砚（清）**
Lotus-leaf ink slab, white jade
(Qing Dynasty, 1644-1911)

箕形砚形同簸箕，砚底一端落地，一端以足支撑，砚面倾斜，便于聚墨。箕形砚流行于唐代。

Dustpan ink slabs had one side resting on desk and a leg on the other side for support, thus making a slope for ink to flow and gather. This shape was popular during the Tang Dynasty.

• **箕形砚（唐）**
Dustpan ink slab (Tang
Dynasty, 618-907)

抄手砚由箕形砚演变而来，砚面一端低，一端高，底挖空，因可用手抄砚底而得名。抄手砚较轻便，始于五代时期，盛行于宋代。

Chao Shou ink slab: It got its name from its unique shape: one side high, the other side low and its bottom hollowed; easily picked up with a hand. Light in weight, this kind first appeared during the Five-dynasty Period and gained popularity during the Song Dynasty.

• **抄手砚（宋）**
Chao Shou ink slab (Song
Dynasty, 960-1279)

圈足砚指砚面呈圆形，以多脚围绕作砚足支撑砚面的砚。砚足的形状有兽蹄、兽首等形状。圈足砚流行于唐代以前，是为了适应当时在矮桌上书写而制作的。

The feeted: round and having multiple feet at the bottom shaped like animal claws or heads. This variety, popular before Tang, was meant for writing on a very low table.

● 圈足砚（唐）
Multiple-feet ink slab (Tang Dynasty, 618-907)

随形砚指因材而制，不在乎砚的轮廓外形，只借助砚材的纹理而创作、雕琢的砚。随形砚奇巧而有灵气，流行甚广，尤以随形扁砚最多，造型千姿百态。

Sui Xing ink slab: Sui Xing meant the slabs made not after anything but the shape and veins of the stone material. This kind was tremendously popular for its unique charm. Of all, the flat ones were majority.

● 歙石金星随形砚（清）
Sui Xing ink slab with golden stars from Shezhou (Qing Dynasty, 1644-1911)

暖砚有两种形式：一种是在墨堂下凿出空腔，灌注热水于内，以保持砚面的温度；另一种是在砚面之下设置底座，底座多为金属制成砚匣，可置炭火以保持温度，金属匣一般都精雕巧作，别具一格。暖砚盛行于明清时期，暖砚砚面多为歙石、端石和松花江石。

Heated ink slabs had two kinds: one had warm water in the hollow under its ink pool to keep warm; the other had an elaborately wrought metal stand at the bottom to keep charcoal. Heated ink slabs, popular during the Qing Dynasty, often used the stones from Shezhou, Duanzhou and the Songhua River.

> 四大名砚

四大名砚之说，最早见于宋人苏易简所著《文房四谱·砚谱》："砚有四十余品，以青州红丝石为第一，端州斧柯山石为第二，歙州龙尾石为第三，甘肃洮河石为第四。"后来，红丝石因开采枯竭而被澄泥砚所取代。

> The Most Famous Four Varieties

This saying, the most famous four, was firstly seen in Su Yijian's book, in its chapter about ink slabs: "Ink slabs are in over forty varieties, but the stone with red threads on it from Qingzhou being the best, the stone from Fuke Mount of Duanzhou the second, the stone from Longwei of Shezhou the third and the stone from the Taohe River of Gansu, the fourth. Later, after the red-thread stone resource was exhausted, the *Cheng*-clay came as its substitute.

红丝砚

红丝砚在宋代居四大名砚之首，产于青州（今山东潍坊、益都、淄博一带），其特点是色泽明艳雅丽，红黄相间，石纹旋曲如波云，石质细润易发墨。红丝石在唐代享有盛名，但到宋代便已采尽，故传世实物极少。宋代苏易简在《文房四谱》中将红丝砚列为第一，是当时最佳的砚品。

The Red-thread Ink Slab

Topping the famous four, this red-thread variety came from Qingzhou (present-day Weifang, Yidu and Zibo), featuring bright colors of red and yellow, with veins twirling and tumbling like clouds, very fine, moistened and ink-friendly. It was taken as a treasure during the Tang Dynasty. However, by the Song Dynasty no more resource was left. Very few exist today. In his book, Su Yijian listed it as the best of all under the heaven.

• 红丝石
The red-thread stone

• 红丝石砚（清）
Red-thread ink slab (Qing Dynasty, 1644-1911)

端砚

端砚因产于端州（今广东肇庆）而得名，最早出现于隋末唐初。端砚石质温润，纹理缜密，贮水不涸，磨之无声，溜不损毫。端砚利于发墨，石品（天然花纹）上佳，经过精雕细琢之后具有极高的艺术价值。

Duan Ink Slabs

This variety got its name from Duanzhou where its material came from (today's Zhaoqing). It was first known during the late Sui (581-618) or the early Tang Deriods(618-907). *Duan* stones featured fine texture and closely knitted veins, very ink-friendly and nice for keeping water. It gave no sound when ink was ground on it. The best about it was its veins, born for being works of art.

- 端石云蝠砚（清）
Duan ink slab with cloud veins, (Qing Dynasty, 1644-1911)

- 端石九眼方砚（清）
Duan ink slab with nine holes (Qing Dynasty, 1644-1911)

端砚的著名石品

石品是划分砚石不同品种的依据之一，端砚的石品通过花纹来鉴别，有以下几种著名石品：

青花　紫色石砚中的最佳品类，其上散布有细小的蓝色花纹或斑点。这些花纹或斑点隐在紫石之中，浸入水中才能看到。

鱼脑冻　砚石中的图案像受冻的鱼脑，有聚有散，洁白如晴天的白云，好像风一吹就要散开，松散如一团柳絮，仿佛一触就要动起来。鱼脑冻是端石精品中最名贵的石品。

蕉叶白　又称"蕉白"，形如蕉叶初展，似含露欲滴，洁白细嫩。蕉叶白四周定有火捺纹（像用火烙过的痕迹），两者相伴而生。蕉叶白石质嫩软细腻，滑如肌肤，利于发墨，是端砚中的上品。

火捺　又称"火烙"，颜色如火烙一般，紫红中带微黑。火捺中最名贵的是金钱火捺，又称"猪肝冻"，色如猪肝，形状为圆形或椭圆形。

天青　指纯洁无杂色、无瑕疵的端石，较为难得。

冰纹　也叫"冰纹冻"，指端石的花纹形状像冰冻裂，属于一般品种。

翡翠　也叫青脉，指砚石表面有绿色圆点或短纹。

绿端　砚石青绿微黄，是端石中非常少见的珍品，易发墨。

荡　指多种品类集于一体的端石。"荡"就是"湖"，湖中多种动植物并生，因此得名。上等荡石里层是鱼脑冻，冻内为青花，冻外是蕉叶白，蕉叶白外是火捺纹围绕。荡石难得一见，是端石中的名贵品种。

Famous Varieties of *Duan* Slabs

Stone quality determined the class of the ink slab. By veins, *Duan* stones had the following varieties:

Qing Hua, or pale green flower, the best of Duan stones. In purple color, it got its name from very fine blue veins or dots only visible in water.

Yu Nao Dong or frozen fish brain, having veins stay together or stay apart, like clouds in sky drifting with wind. This variety was the rarest in Duan stones.

Jiao Ye Bai or fresh banana leaf: this variety got its name from its veins like fresh and tender banana leaves; around the veins were marks like left by fire. This variety gave a very tender and fine look, like woman's beautiful skin. Also ink-friendly, this variety was a very expensive kind in the Duan stone family.

Huo Nai or marks left by fire: dark purple, almost black. The rarest stone in this variety was called pig's liver stone in round or oval shape.

Tian Qing or heavenly blue: the stones without any flaw in it, very rare to get.

Bing Wen or ice vein: having veins like tiny seams from freezing, a common variety.

Fei Cui or emerald: also called the blue vein, having green dots or short veins on surface.

Lv Duan or green ends: pale green, a bit yellowish, very rare in the Duan family, also ink-friendly.

Dang: referring to a stone having all kinds of veins mentioned above on surface, one next to another like a lake overgrown with varieties of plants in and around it. This variety was very rare.

• 鱼脑冻砚（清）

鱼脑冻因砚石中的图案像受冻的鱼脑而得名，是端石精品中的精品。

Yu Nao Dong ink slab (Qing Dynasty, 1644-1911)

It got the name because the pattern is like some frozen fish brain. This piece is the best of the best Duan style ink slabs.

歙砚

歙砚也称"龙尾砚",唐代始有,因砚石产于歙州(今江西婺源一带)而得名。歙砚石的特点是石色青莹,纹理细密,发墨既快速,又细润。歙砚因其石组织结构聚结紧密,自然孔隙小,故具有发墨益毫、滑不拒墨、涩不滞笔、贮墨久而不涸的特点。

She Ink Slabs

She ink slabs were also called *Long Wei* or the tail of dragon slabs, first seen during the Tang Dynasty. They got their name from the stones quarried in Shezhou (present-day Wuyuan of Jiangxi Province). The stones from there were in a very pleasant color, very solid and very fine in texture, moistened and ink friendly. Because of their solid texture the natural holes they had were exceptionally tiny, able to keep ink for a long time.

- 歙砚(现代)
  The *She* ink slab (contemporary product)

李煜与龙尾砚

传说李煜有一方龙尾砚,色如青绿,润如秋月,砚池中有个黄色的石弹丸,一年三百六十日,水都不会干涸。而且有一只小青蛙头露水面,每到夜深人静时,蛙声如鼓,伴李煜弹琴作画。李煜视其为珍宝,爱不释手。

宋太祖八年(975)宋军攻破金陵(今江苏南京),李煜被俘,并被押解到汴京(今河南开封)。李煜仅携带了此砚,相传他用此砚研出的墨汁,写出了"问君能有几多愁,恰似一江春水向东流"的千古佳句。

Li Yu and "Dragon-tail Ink Slab"

The "dragon-tail" ink slab Li Yu had, as the legend says, was in a very pleasant pale green color like the autumn moon. In the middle of the ink pool was a yellow stone, which never dried up throughout a year. A small fog appeared from the slab at midnight to croak, to keep Li Yu's company while the latter was painting or playing a musical instrument. Li Yu hated to part with it for a single moment.

Yet he was captured when the Song army took Jinling, present-day Nanjing, in the eighth year of the Tai Zu Reign (975). He brought nothing along with him except for this ink slab, with which, he wrote the most famous lines of his, "Asked how much sorrow I have, it is like the east-bound torrential water in the Yangtze, I said."

● 龙尾砚
The dragon-tail ink slab

洮河砚

洮河砚又叫"绿石砚"，因产于洮州（今甘肃临潭）而得名。洮河石深埋于大河深水之底，因山陡水险，气候冷，不易开采，洮州又远居陇上，交通不便，所以洮河砚在明清时期已属珍品。洮河石属沉积岩，质细色美，发墨快，温润无

Tao He Ink Slabs

The *Tao He* ink slabs had another name, "green stone ink slabs". They got the name from the place the stone was quarried, Taozhou (present-day Lintan of Gansu), from the bottom of the deep Taohe River. Quarrying was very difficult because of the cold weather, torrential waves and difficult transportation. Even

比，可呵气成珠，以其制成的砚，余墨贮于其中经月不涸，亦不变质，前人有"端州歙州无此色"的说法。

during the Qing Dynasty the ink slabs made with this *Tao He* stone were rare. This stone, a sedimentary kind, had very fine texture in a beautiful look, perfect for grinding ink upon. Also, its moist surface was said able to turn exhaled air instantly into water drops. Ink in it wouldn't dry after months. No wonder people said, "This ink slab has no match in this by any from either Duanzhou or Shezhou " .

* 洮河石砚（清）
Tao He ink slab (Qing Dynasty, 1644-1911)

文天祥与洮河砚

文天祥（1236—1283），南宋时期的爱国将领，著名诗人。在强敌入侵，国土沦陷的危急时刻，他变卖家产，组织义军英勇抗敌，最后慷慨就义。

文天祥有一方绿色的洮河砚，这方砚受墨之处微凹，底圆而凸，形如蝉腹。沿左边至顶，刻有谢皋羽的铭文，并留有款识"皋羽"二字。文天祥去世后，此砚不知去向。

清代乾隆丁未年（1787）十二月，杭州一个渔夫在临平湖捕鱼时无意间网得一方砚。文人王仲瞿乘舟经过，观砚后认定为文天祥之物，当即买下后赠于友人袁枚。袁枚特制一个檀香木匣，用以放置此砚，并在匣上刻文记述获砚经过。

* 文天祥像
Wen Tianxiang

Wen Tianxiang and His *Tao He* Ink Slab

Wen Tianxiang (1236-1283), army general of the Southern Song Dynasty, also a famed poet. Before the invading army he sold all of his properties and with the money he grouped an army to fight until he was killed.

He had a green *Tao He* ink slab lower in the middle for ink to gather, its bottom protruding like the belly of a cicada going all the way from left to top. Xie Gaoyu's inscription was seen with his name at the bottom. After Wen Tianxiang's death this ink slab was lost.

One day in December of 1787 during the Qian Long Reign of the the Qing Dynasty, a fisherman netted an ink slab from the bottom of the Linping Lake. It so happened that scholar Wang Zhongqu was passing in a boat. He concluded it from Wen Tianxiang. So he bought it from the fisherman. He later gave it as a gift to his friend Yuan Mei, who cased it in a sandalwood box and inscribed the top about how this treasure had been retrieved.

• 洮河石长方砚（明）
Rectangular *Tao He* ink slab
(Ming Dynasty, 1368-1644)

澄泥砚

澄泥砚是陶砚中的精品，后取代红丝砚成中国四大名砚之一。澄泥砚始于晋唐之间，早于端砚、歙砚。澄泥砚产于山西省绛县，具有细腻坚实、滋润胜水、历寒不冰、发墨不损毫的特点，能与石质佳砚相媲美。

澄泥砚是将细河泥经过仔细淘洗、过滤后逐渐沉淀于袋中，经年

Cheng-clay Ink Slabs

A pottery variety, the *Cheng*-clay ink slab replaced the famous red-thread to be one of the famous four. First seen during the Jin Dynasty or the Tang Dynasty, earlier than the birth of *Duan* or She slabs, the *Cheng*-clay ink slabs made in the Jiangxian County, Shanxi, were solid in texture, pleasantly moistened and never froze even in the coldest weather. Though clay, they were as good as stone ones.

后取出后风干，再掺进黄丹团后用力揉搓，放入模具成型，然后用竹刀雕琢，干燥后放进窑内烧，最后裹上黑蜡烧制而成。

澄泥砚因原料来源、烧制时间的不同，而具有鳝鱼黄、蟹壳青、绿豆砂、玫瑰紫、豆瓣砂、朱砂等不同颜色。澄泥砚一般注重图案，讲究造型，雕砚刀笔凝练，技艺精湛，状物摹态形象毕肖、灵通活脱。

Fine river mud was washed, rinsed and sieved repeatedly before it accumulated in a cloth bag. Years later, after the mud was air-dried yellow lead was added, and the mixture was kneaded until it was ready for molding. After receiving decoration by a bamboo cutter, it was air-dried, coated with black wax and fired in a kiln.

Because of different places the clay came from and also because of different time of kilning, the *Cheng*-clay ink slabs took different colors, yellow, pale green, purple or red, very impressive after carving. Every image carved was exquisite and life-like.

● 荷叶鲤鱼澄泥砚（现代）
Lotus and carp *Cheng*-clay ink slab (contemporary product)

● 九龙澄泥砚（现代）
Nine-dragon *Cheng*-clay ink slab (contemporary product)

古砚的保养

砚在中国历史悠久，古代中国人在使用过程中已形成了很好的收藏和保存砚的方法。

仔细洗砚：砚使用后，应随时洗涤，不能留墨，以免因墨干燥龟裂而损坏砚面。洗砚要用清水和皂角水，不可用碱水，因碱水有微腐蚀性，久用会使砚石变得平光而无法发墨。洗砚时将砚置于木盆内（不能用水泥盆、瓷盆洗涤，以免碰伤砚），用经水泡软后的丝瓜瓤或莲房壳慢慢洗涤，这样既能洗去墨垢，又不伤砚。

古人认为长期洗涤的砚，时间一久，还会出现轻微的光泽，流露出一种古雅之色，这就是行家们所珍视的"包浆"。

以水养砚：砚洗干净以后，还得用清水保养。将洗涤干净的砚取出风干，然后放于砚匣内。在砚池中注入清水，每日一换，以养砚之莹润。

以匣藏砚：藏砚最好用木制的砚匣。

注意避光：藏砚一定要注意避光，否则砚质易干燥，也易使砚匣干裂。

- 带盒长方形端砚（清）
Cased rectangular *Duan* ink slab (Qing Dynasty, 1644-1911)

The Keeping of Ancient Ink Slabs

Over the past thousands of years Chinese people had developed an effective way to keep ink slabs out of harm's way.

Washed carefully after use: after being used, an ink slab should be washed clean immediately. No ink should be left after use, which might dry up to damage the slab. Washing should be done with clean water plus saponin, no water containing soda to be used because it was erosive and after a period of time the ink slab might become glossy and resistant against ink. Washing should be done inside a wood basin (no hard basin like porcelain or cement because damage may happen from knocks). Using vegetable sponge or lotus seed pot and do washing gently. That soft stuff gets rid of ink effectively and leaves no stain.

After years of washing in a right way, ancient people believed, ink slabs might take on a shimmering look, something only antiques had. Experts called this change *Bao Jiang*.

Use water to moisten ink slabs: after being washed clean fresh water is used for further care. Then, the slab is left to air-dry before back to its case. A little fresh water should be left in its ink pool and changed every day.

Use a case to keep it: Wood cases are the best.

Keep them out of the sun: this is important. Otherwise, ink slabs may dry and the case crack.

• 三星五福石砚（清）

Ink slab with Three Stars upon Five Bats
Pattern (An auspicious design implied
wealth, longevity, luck and happiness)
(Qing Dynasty, 1644-1911)

附录：其他文房用具
Appendix: Other Tools in a Traditional Chinese Study

笔筒

用于盛放毛笔的筒状物，形状多样，以圆筒状最为常见，外壁常雕刻精美纹饰。笔筒的材质很多，有竹、木、象牙、玉石、瓷、雕漆、金属等。

Writing Brush Container

Containers for writing brushes were in different shapes but the most common was cylindrical, often carved on their outside walls. They were made with materials like bamboo, wood, ivory, jade, marble, porcelain, lacquer or metal.

- 竹雕梅花笔筒（明）
Bamboo brush container with plum blossoms (Ming Dynasty, 1368-1644)

- 紫檀云龙笔筒（清）
Rosewood brush container with cloud and dragon (Qing Dynasty, 1644-1911)

- 黄釉竹节雕春牛图笔筒（清）

Yellow glazed bamboo joint brush container with ox (Qing Dynasty, 1644-1911)

- 碧玉九老图笔筒（清）

Jade brush container with sages (Qing Dynasty, 1644-1911)

- 象牙雕笔筒（清）

Carved ivory brush container (Qing Dynasty, 1644-1911)

- 蓝上蓝福寿开光墨彩花鸟纹海棠式笔筒（清）

Glazed crabapple blue brush container with auspicious images (Qing Dynasty, 1644-1911)

- 粉彩开光石纹笔筒（清）
Color stone brush container (Qing Dynasty, 1644-1911)

- 牛骨雕笔筒（现代）
Carved ox bone brush container (contemporary product)

笔架

　　用于临时搁放毛笔的文房用具。使用毛笔时，因笔头蘸有墨，在放下时需保证笔头悬空，不会来回滚动，笔架因此而诞生。笔架没有固定的形状，一般多为三峰或多峰，有的钻有透孔。

Writing Brush Rack

For temporary rest of writing brushes. When a brush tip had ink on it must be placed without touching anything when temporarily out of use. The rack was also to prevent a brush from rolling on the desk. Brush racks had no fixed shape, but often made for three or more brushes. Some had holes.

- 青花笔架（明）
Blue-and-white brush rack (Ming Dynasty, 1368-1644)

- 白玉笔架（清）
White jade brush rack (Qing Dynasty, 1644-1911)

- 青玉凤凰松树笔架（清）
Gray jade brush rack with phoenix and
pine tree (Qing Dynasty, 1644-1911)

- 青玉鹿纹笔架（清）
Gray jade deer brush rack (Qing
Dynasty, 1644-1911)

- 五峰铜笔架（清）
Five-peak copper brush rack (Qing
Dynasty, 1644-1911)

- 青花五峰笔架（清）
Blue-and-white five-peak brush rack
(Qing Dynasty, 1644-1911)

- 黄杨木天然笔架（清）
Boxwood brush rack (Qing Dynasty ,
1644-1911)

笔洗

洗毛笔的容器。古人用毛笔蘸墨写字，因墨中含有胶，墨干后会把毛笔的毛粘住，再用水泡开时，会损伤毛笔。所以一般不用毛笔时，都在笔洗中把毛笔洗净。绘画时因为使用墨、颜料的不同，也要用笔洗，所以笔洗是不可缺少的文具。

笔洗形制奇巧，样式繁多，多为大口或敞口的浅容器，常见的有荷叶式、贝叶式、葵瓣式、蕉叶式、瓜式、葫芦式、风式等样式的笔洗。

Writing Brush Washer

It is a container for washing brushes. Because ink contained glue that held the brush hairs together when the ink was dry, damage may happen to brush tips. Each time after use the brush tip had to be washed very clean—the same with tips having paints. Therefore, writing brush washers became indispensible.

These washers might be in different forms but most of them had a big opening on top. They were shaped like lotus, pattra, sunflower, banana leaf, a melon or a gourd.

• 青玉福寿花形洗（明）
Gray jade flower writing brush washer with longevity and happiness symbols (Ming Dynasty, 1368-1644)

• 墨玉椭圆梅花洗（明）
Black jade oval plum writing brush washer (Ming Dynasty, 1368-1644)

• 青玉叶形洗（明）
Gray jade leaf writing brush washer (Ming Dynasty, 1368-1644)

• 仿痕玉活环菊花洗（清）
Jade chrysanthemum writing brush washer (Qing Dynasty, 1644-1911)

- 白玉荷叶洗（清）
  White jade lotus leaf writing brush washer (Qing Dynasty, 1644-1911)

- 白玉荷莲笔洗（清）
  White jade lotus leaf writing brush washer (Qing Dynasty, 1644-1911)

笔掭

　　古代文人用来掭拭毛笔的用具。古人在书写绘画时，有时笔头会有不顺，或有含墨过多的情况，在下笔之前可在笔掭上进行调试，为下笔行文描色作更好的准备。笔掭有瓷、玉、琉璃、水晶等材质。

Writing Brush Tester

Before either writing or painting, ancient people used a tester to try the brush tip or the amount of ink it contained, to make sure the hairs were neat and orderly and the ink amount was right, neither too much or too little. This was a tool to avoid inconsistency in shades. Common materials for the testers included porcelain, jade, colored glaze or crystal.

- 白釉荷叶式笔掭（五代）
  White glazed lotus leaf writing brush tester (Five Dynasty Period, 907-960)

- 仿官窑笔掭（清）
  Tester, imitation of product from an official kiln (Qing Dynasty, 1644-1911)

• 象牙笔抿（清）
Ivory writing brush tester (Qing Dynasty, 1644-1911)

笔床

　　用来卧放毛笔的用具，在性能上相当于笔盒。笔床有镏金、翡翠、瓷、紫檀、乌木等材质，现在能见到的笔床多为瓷和竹木制品。

Writing Brush Bed

The tool that writing brushes "sleep" upon, similar in function as a brush box. Common materials for the bed included porcelain, emerald, rosewood and ebony. Some were gold plated. Most of the beds we can see today are either porcelain, bamboo or wooden.

• 青花描金粉彩山水开光人物纹笔床（清）
Blue-and-white, gold-traced, patterned writing brush bed with landscape and human figure (Qing Dynasty, 1644-1911)

墨床

　　古人在研磨墨停顿下来时，用来放墨锭的文房用具。研墨停顿时，墨锭一头沾有墨汁，若随意放很容易弄脏别处，墨床就用来临时搁置墨锭。墨床的体积不大，多以小巧秀美取胜。常见的墨床形状包括几形、多宝槅形、盒形等。

Ink Bed

For temporary rest of an ink stick between grindings. One end of the stick had ink juice. To avoid a mess on the desk this ink stick bed came into being. Usually, the bed was small, but very exquisite and attractive at looks. Common appearances included geometric forms, a shelf in ancient style or simply a box.

- 白玉俎式墨床（清）
  White jade ink stick bed (Qing Dynasty, 1644-1911)

- 水晶墨床（清）
  Crystal ink stick bed (Qing Dynasty, 1644-1911)

- 黄玛瑙竹节式墨床（清）
  Yellow agate bamboo-joint ink stick bed (Qing Dynasty, 1644-1911)

- 白玉墨床（清）
  White jade ink stick bed (Qing Dynasty, 1644-1911)

书镇

又名"镇纸",是压纸张的用具,其功能一是防止纸被风吹走,二是可以把纸抻平,便于写字作画。有的镇纸做成尺子的形状,所以又名"镇尺"。镇纸集实用性与观赏性于一体,造型变化多样,但不论造型如何,都有底部平整、重心低、有一定的重量、表面光洁四个基本特点。

Book Weight

Also called paper weight, something to keep paper from being blown away by wind. It had another function: keep paper smooth for writing and painting. Some paperweights were made like a ruler. No matter in what appearance they were both practical in use and beautiful to look at. They should have a very flat and smooth bottom, low center of gravity, weighty and smooth on surface.

- 铜狮镇纸（清）
  Copper lion paperweight (Qing Dynasty, 1644-1911)

- 青玉天鹅形镇纸（清）
  Gray jade swan paperweight (Qing Dynasty, 1644-1911)

- 青玉"三阳开泰"镇纸（清）
  Gray jade paperweight with auspicious symbols (Qing Dynasty, 1644-1911)

- 翡翠圆形镇纸（清）
  Emerald round paperweight (Qing Dynasty, 1644-1911)

- 紫檀木嵌竹刻书镇（现代）
Rosewood inlaid with bamboo inscription paperweight(contemporary product)

- 竹雕镇纸（现代）
Inscribed bamboo paperweight (contemporary product)

臂搁

　　用来搁手臂的一种文房用具，在宋代就已出现。古人写毛笔字的顺序是从右往左，从上往下，在换行的时候手腕正好在刚写好的字上，容易把字蹭花，把衣服弄脏，臂搁的制作与使用解决了这一问题。臂搁上常雕饰花纹，有很高的观赏价值。

Arm Pillow

It was first seen during the Song Dynasty (960-1279). Ancient people wrote from right to left and from top to bottom. When they were changing a line their wrist was just above the characters freshly written, easily destroyed them and stained their sleeves. Arm pillows solved this problem. These pillows often beautifully carved, were works of art.

- 青玉竹节臂搁（明）
Gray jade bamboo-joint arm pillow (Ming Dynasty, 1368-1644)

- 翡翠臂搁（清）
Emerald arm pillow (Qing Dynasty, 1644-1911)

● 留青竹刻荷塘纹臂搁（清）

Arm pillow inscribed with bamboo (Qing Dynasty, 1644-1911)

● 平刻象牙婴戏图臂搁（现代）

Ivory arm pillow inscribed with children (contemporary product)

● 留青花鸟纹竹雕臂搁（清）

Arm pillow with flower, bird and bamboo (Qing Dynasty, 1644-1911)

● 象牙雕臂搁（现代）

Ivory inscribed arm pillow (contemporary product)

砚滴

又称"水注"，是向砚里注水的工具，在西晋已较为流行，宋元时期盛行。砚滴一般做成青蛙、乌龟、瑞兽的形状，摆设在书桌上，也极具观赏价值。尽管砚滴的外形多种多样，但有三点结构是共同的：一是腹内中空，可以盛水；二是在较高的位置上有一细孔，倾倒时，可以滴出水来；三是背上有一个圆孔和腹相同，圆孔上有一段高起的管状器，可以注入水，用水时，用一个手指按住，把砚滴移到砚台上时，不会有水洒出，只要略松开手指，便有水滴到砚台上。

Ink Slab Water Filler

A tool that fills water into an ink slab already seen during the Western Jin Dynasty (265-316) but popular in the later Song (960-1279) and the Yuan Dynastyies (1279-1368). It was often shaped after a frog, a turtle or some legendary animal, something to be placed on a desk. Apart from its practical use it was pleasant to look at. They shared three common features: hollow inside to keep water, having a small hole on upper part for water to outflow, having another hole on top attached to a tube for filling. Keep a finger on this hole before the filler is moved to the ink slab and remove the finger so water drips onto the ink slab.

笔墨纸砚
Writing Brush, Ink Stick, Paper and Ink Slab

• 越窑兔形砚滴（三国）
Hare filler from a *Yue* kiln (Three Kingdom Period, 220-280)

• 青瓷兔形水注（晋）
Celadon hare filler (Jin Dynasty, 265-420)

• 玉兽形砚滴（宋）
Jade filler in an animal shape (Song Dynasty, 960-1279)

• 青白釉凤首流水注（宋）
Glazed pale green filler with a phoenix head (Song Dynasty, 960-1279)

• 青玉卧凤砚滴（明）
Pale green jade phoenix filler (Ming Dynasty, 1368-1644)

• 龙泉窑舟形砚滴（元）
Boat filler from *Longquan* Kiln (Yuan Dynasty, 1279-1368)

- 宣德款龟形铜砚滴（明）
  Copper turtle filler in Xuande style (Ming Dynasty, 1368-1644)

- 铜蟾形砚滴（明）
  Copper toad filler (Ming Dynasty, 1368-1644)

水盂

　　又称"水丞"，小型盛水器皿，磨墨时就用小匙从中舀出水来。水盂体形小巧，做工精致，一般配有铜或珊瑚制成的匙。水盂的样式很多，有方形、圆形、海棠形、如意形、桃形、荷叶形、葫芦形、荷叶莲蓬型、鹅形、鸭形、蟾形、海螺形等，口有圆口、葵口、菱口、花口等。

Water Jar

Use a small spoon to bail water out of this jar for grinding ink. Usually the jar was small but very exquisitely made, often having a copper or coral key on one side. It had different shapes, square or round or fashioned after auspicious plants, animals or birds. Their openings varied a lot in shape and in size.

- 青釉蛙形水盂（西晋）
  Pale green glazed frog jar (Western Jin Dynasty, 265-316)

- 水晶桃式水盂（明）
  Crystal peach jar (Ming Dynasty, 1368-1644)

• 天蓝釉小水盂（清）
Azure-blue glazed small jar (Qing Dynasty, 1644-1911)

• 玛瑙荷叶水丞（清）
Agate lotus leaf jar (Qing Dynasty, 1644-1911)

• 铜童戏水盂（清）
Copper jar of children playing with water (Qing Dynasty, 1644-1911)

• 宜兴窑双螭福寿水丞（清）
Jar kilned in Yixing, with legendary dragons standing for happiness and longevity (Qing Dynasty, 1644-1911)

• 青玉秋蝉桐叶水丞（清）
Pale jade cicada and tung-leaf jar (Qing Dynasty, 1644-1911)

• 清代紫晶玉兰花水丞（清）
Amethyst magnolia flower jar (Qing Dynasty, 1644-1911)

《中国红》出版编辑委员会

主　　任　　王亚非

副 主 任　　田海明　林清发

编　　委　　（以姓氏笔划为序）

王亚非　　毛白鸽　　田海明　　包云鸠

孙建君　　任耕耘　　吕　军　　吕品田

吴　鹏　　杜国新　　林清发　　赵国华

徐　雯　　涂卫中　　唐元明　　韩　进

蒋一谈

执行编委　　任耕耘　　蒋一谈

中国酒
Chinese Wine

古钱币
Ancient Coins

刺绣
Chinese Embroidery

中国禅
Zen

棋艺
Art of Chesses

中国节日
Chinese Festivals

中国饮食
Chinese Food

中国名湖
Famous Lakes in China

中国料器
Chinese Glassware

帝王陵寝
Imperial Mausoleum

中华传统美德
Chinese Traditional Virtues

中国姓氏
Chinese Surnames

传统家具
Chinese Furniture

中国名山
Renowned Chinese Mountains

中国染织
Chinese Dyeing and Weaving

中国雕刻
Chinese Sculpture

少数民族服饰
Wears of Chinese Minorities

古代教育
Education in Ancient China

中国神话传说
Chinese Mythology and Legends

古代游戏
Recreational Games in Ancient China

四大名著
Four Masterpieces of Chinese Fiction

古代科技
Ancient China's Science and Technology

梅兰竹菊
Plum Blossom, Orchid, Bamboo and Chrysanthemum

竹木牙角器
Art Crafts Make of Bamboo, Wood, Ivory and Horn

风筝
Kites

盆景
Bonsai

景泰蓝
Cloisonné

泥塑
Clay Sculpture

面塑
Dough Figuring

大运河
Grand Canal

历史名城
Historical Cities

中国结
Chinese Knots

兵马俑
Terracotta Army

皮影
Folk Shadow Play

中国古代帝王
Emperors of China

中国陶器
Chinese Pottery Ware

中国漆器
Chinese Lacquer Articles

中国名寺
Famous Temples in China

中国石窟
Grottoes in China

中国古桥
Ancient Bridges in China

中国古塔
Ancient Pagodas in China

中国民居
Traditional Civil Residents

民间戏曲
Traditional Folk Operas

中国灯彩
Colorful Chinese Lanterns and Lamps

诸子百家
Traditional Philosophers and Ideologists

中国牌坊
Chinese Decorated and Memorial Archways

中国茶艺
Chinese Tea Appreciation Ceremony

秦砖汉瓦
Brick of Qin Dynasty and Tile of Han Dynasty

面具
Masks

鼻烟壶
Snuff Bottles

颐和园
The Summer Palace

丝绸之路
The Silk Road

汉字
Chinese Characters

中国木偶艺术
Chinese Puppet Arts

古代兵书
Ancient Book on the Art of War

道教文化
Daoism Culture in China

古代交通
Ancient Traffic

古代壁画
Ancient Chinese Mural Painting

古代衡器
Ancient Weighing Apparatus

24节气
The Twenty-four Solar Terms

中国名泉
Famous Springs in China

长江黄河
Yangtze River and Yellow River

传统杂技
Traditional Acrobatic Arts

中国婚俗
Marriage Customs in China

匾额对联
Inscribed Tablets and Couplets

中国建筑装饰
Chinese Architectural Decoration

十二生肖
The Twelve Animals Represent Years

佩饰
Ornaments Wore by Ancient Chinese

文房清供
Stationery and Bibelot in Ancient Studies

中国祥禽瑞兽
Auspicious Beasts and Fowls in Chinese Culture